To Linda,
Hope you w.) y
the read.
Monica

WATS, WADIS
and WATERFALLS

*A Canadian Woman's Travel and
Teaching Experiences in the Middle
East and Southeast Asia*

MONICA MURPHY

 FriesenPress

One Printers Way
Altona, MB R0G 0B0
Canada

www.friesenpress.com

Edited by Ginny Jaques

ISBN
978-1-03-918331-5 (Hardcover)
978-1-03-918330-8 (Paperback)
978-1-03-918332-2 (eBook)

1. BIOGRAPHY & AUTOBIOGRAPHY, PERSONAL MEMOIRS

Distributed to the trade by The Ingram Book Company

WATS, WADIS *and* WATERFALLS

To David,
thanks for being part of the adventure!

Introduction

At the tender age of fifty, with no Chinese money and no Chinese language, Monica found herself walking with a man she didn't know on a Chinese street after midnight. Having taken a one-week course in teaching, she tried to find a teaching job in or around Vancouver, but was unable to find job locally.

So she started selling small classified ads for a community newspaper. One day, her eyes strayed to the employment section of the paper. There was an ad for teachers in China. They were asking for a three- or four-year degree, and she had a three-year diploma in Travel and Tourism. She had always wanted to travel and live in another country and this was her chance! She walked over to the fax machine and faxed the school a copy of her resume. The recruiter, Elaine, called her the next day and ten days later she was on a plane on her way to Guangzhou China! By midnight of that day, she had met her first new "Friend."

Monica Murphy
English Teacher
BA- General Studies
MA- Education

Ph-(095) 09-260024934
monicateacher@hotmail.com
monicateacher2003@yahoo.com
monicamurphy347@gmail.com

Business Card

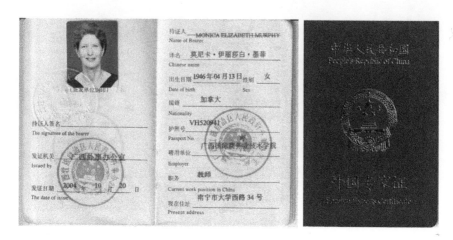

My Foreign Expert's Certificate

Chapter One

Arrival in China

Just ten days after I saw the ad for English teachers at a school in China, on my day of departure, the phone rang. I thought it was the woman I was going to work for but she had a strange request.

"Have you got the lumber?" She repeated this again.

This took me aback at first, and then I realized she meant the number of the school that she and her husband owned, and the word "number" was difficult for her. As it turned out, it was a good thing I had the number when I finally arrived in China.

I had recently taken a one-week course in teaching, but I was unable to find a job locally, so I applied at a small community newspaper to sell small classified ads. This was one of the many telemarketing sales jobs I had worked at over the last ten years, even though I had a three-year diploma in travel and tourism. This qualification turned out to be basically useless, and BCIT wouldn't give me any credit for my studies to complete their program. So I worked on the phone, selling everything from ad space to cruises. (I got a trip to Florida for that one).

But-this was not what I wanted to do with my life, and I had always wanted to travel and live in another country. While I was looking for small ads to contact, my eyes strayed to the employment section of the newspaper. There was an ad for teachers in China! They were asking for a three or four-year degree. I walked over to the fax machine and faxed them my resume, which I just happened to have with me in the hopes that this would change my life. And it did! They called me the next day, I had an interview with a very chic woman from Taiwan, and started packing.

My flight was from Vancouver to Hong Kong, connecting with a one-hour flight to Guangzhou, (Gwanjo). I was told that someone from the airport would meet me and escort me to the ensuing flight.

After a ten- hour night flight with no sleep (night flight), we arrived in Hong Kong. There was a big sign in English, among the many Chinese signs waving in the air, with my name on it. As there was only one hour between flights the woman holding the sign grabbed my hand and told me to run, as there was such a short time before takeoff.

We made it just before they closed the doors. Were they waiting for me? Getting settled, I breathed a deep sigh of relief as I started to relax.

I've always been an adventurous sort of person, and the chance to fly halfway around the world to a new country made me more excited than apprehensive. I reflected on what this adventure would bring to my life.

After all, what could possibly go wrong? A big city of seven million people was bound to have lots of English-speaking people, and, as far as teaching went, I did have a certificate from The Canadian Institute of English, for the one-week course I had taken. At the tender age of 50, I was ready for a new start.

Back home, my family members had varied reactions to my new adventure. My father, a former airline pilot, thought it was great, but my mother, one of those over-protective worry-warts, cried out when I showed her a copy of my contract. The heading at the top was "The People's Republic of China," and this frightened her. A former news editor, she tended to believe whatever she read in the papers. My son David had given me a Chinese/English electronic translator, which worked fine for a while, but the replacement batteries were fiendishly expensive.

Thoughts of family were interrupted by an announcement on the PA system. It was in the Chinese cadence, and it took a few seconds to realize the announcement was in English! I could only pick up a word here and there, and I started to think this adventure might not be so much fun after all.

At that time (1996), the airport was in the city, and as we flew past the high-rises we could see people eating dinner in their apartments. We landed quickly, and I put my carry-on bag on my shoulder. They had told me they were keeping my big suitcase in Hong Kong to x-ray it.

I scanned the crowd of people meeting the plane, and scanned it again for my name. It wasn't there! Bleary-eyed and bone-weary, I sat on a bench to wait for my ride.

"I'll just wait here for a couple of minutes until someone comes to pick me up," I thought.

Soon a Chinese girl came up and asked if she could help me find a hotel.

"No, someone is coming to meet me, and I'm fine. I'm just going to wait here for a little while."

"Oh, no, you can't do that. We're closing the airport!"

Closing the airport?

So I walked out on the street, surrounded by hordes of people, and a voice in my ear said, "Can I take your bag?"

"No, I'm fine," I said, as I clutched the straps tighter.

He reassured me. "It's okay."

Something about that man made me trust him. He asked what I needed and I said I wanted to call my school. He took me to a small hotel and made (and paid for) the call. I had no Chinese money and no

Chinese language. After my long flight I really needed the bathroom. I tried to ask for a bathroom while the man was in another room making the call, but the staff didn't understand any of my English words. I tried bathroom, ladies' room, WC, and even used sign language to indicate a squat, but all were met with blank stares.

Fortunately, the man returned quickly and informed me that the director of the school would be coming to pick me up. This was just one of the many kindnesses shown to me by the Chinese people. I should have got his name or number.

Andrew finally showed up, very apologetic, with a couple of the Chinese TAs. He explained that His mother had recently died, and there was a ceremony. (I was told that he had gasped when someone reminded him I was coming.)

I kept staring out the car window at the show outside. It was close to midnight, and the streets were alive with cars, bicycles, and walkers. All the stores were open. People were getting haircuts, buying clothes and EATING. I had read in the guidebook that in Guangzhou people eat everything that runs, swims, flies or crawls. Bars were open on the sidewalks. People were eating barbecues.

"Everything is interesting, isn't it!" one of the girls commented.

No wonder Asians find Vancouver boring! Most businesses close at 6 pm in Vancouver!

When we reached the hotel I was told I could rest the next day and I gratefully closed the door, took a welcoming bath and crawled into bed. I was just drifting off when there was a loud banging on the door. One of the girls told me she wanted to take me to a place where I could get some breakfast. I said, "No!" as I was in bed and would pick something up in the morning.

She said, "Yes!" because they have Western type muffins and coffee. After some more arguing back and forth I got up, followed her to the Pearl Hotel and the deli. This was my introduction to China.

The next day the girls took me to my apartment to drop off my things, then to the school. I was told to wait downstairs at the front door of the apartment and a taxi would pick me up. The front and back entrance looked exactly alike to me and I couldn't read Chinese characters. It took me a long time to figure out which was the back and which was the front.

My two roommates, Peggy and Martin were both Canadian-- Peggy from Penticton BC, and Martin from Montreal. He had gone to university with the Trudeaus and liked them. Peggy had been in China for two years and Martin was new, like me.

The apartment was very new and fully furnished, but it only had a 4-burner hotplate in the kitchen. No oven. I learned that the Chinese don't use convection ovens, but it didn't stop them from making delicious meals, though. It was amazing to see how the Chinese people could create such delicious meals without fancy dishes or kitchen machines. They would cook soup in a rice cooker and then use it for rice.

Peggy didn't want to help us new teachers, as she taught all day and didn't want more teaching at the end of the day. She moved upstairs with some other girls and we were on our own. So there we were, all alone in a beautiful high-rise apartment, listening to the howling of the dogs in the zoo below. We joked about ordering pizza. Take-out meals weren't available in those days.

We went out to dinner that night and were handed a menu all in Chinese characters! When the waiter saw we didn't understand it he motioned Martin to go outside with him. Outside? Well, the live-animal cages were out there, including cats, and people would choose their fresh dinner without a menu. There were no dogs in cages because dog meat was sold in special restaurants.

When Martin came back he said he didn't know what we were getting, but when he was shown the snakes he waved his arms and shouted, "No!" A couple of minutes later a dish was brought to us. The waiter removed the lid with a great flourish, and there it was, neatly coiled in a circle. We did eat the snake and it was tasty. Good to keep an open mind!

A few weeks later I went out to dinner with another man, Harry, who taught at the Science University and helped me a lot. He became a friend. A waiter brought the paper bag to the table that seemed to be moving. He showed it to Harry who nodded, and took it away. I asked what that was all about. "Oh, they just wanted to show me that the fish was still alive!"

Harry and Family, including his 94-year-old Mother!

The Schools

My first school was called "Sesame Street," based on the tv program. The kids loved it, especially the games. However, their grandparents would come and glare through the windows. Grandparents are very involved with their grandchildren in China.

After about a month, Andrew called me and said he wanted to come and see me after work. "Good news or bad?" I half- jokingly said, and he said, "It depends." He never showed up, but my classes were gradually taken away from me until I had none. Martin stayed out late one Friday night, even though Saturday was a working day, and didn't answer his phone the next morning. He was still sleeping it off. Since I didn't have any classes I went out for the day and joined the Hash Harriers, a running/walking social group. When I got home later that day I couldn't get in because Andrew had changed the locks.

My mother sent me a very negative article about this company which mentioned that they went through 300 teachers in 3 years, and some teachers were even fired for not being good looking enough!

One of the teachers gave me the phone number of another school. I started teaching corporate clients on a part time basis. They gave me a room in a guest house that was in the same building as our school. One place we went to often was P & G (Proctor and Gamble). I always knew we were getting close by the smell of soap. Once when I took the bus in the evening that went a different route all the workers on the bus yelled at me when we reached my stop.

This reminded me of a similar incident in Vancouver when there was an Asian boy on the bus. You had to step down on the back step to activate the back door, and he didn't know what to do. The bus wouldn't move if someone was getting off, so everyone was yelling, "Step down!" but he just looked embarrassed and confused until someone showed him in sign language.

After working in Guangzhou for a few months I was offered a job an hour out of the city in Shun De, which was still part of the countryside. The contract offered me free accommodation and more money, so I moved out to the country. They weren't worried about credentials, and I think I was hired because of my foreign face. (photo of school)

All the teachers lived on the seventh floor, and I got into pretty good shape from going up and down three or four times a day. I could manage the stairs but the day I arrived I was worried about how I was going to get my suitcases up there. I was told "Oh, don't worry, the workers will do it. The "workers" turned out to be tiny women, half my size and height, but they were stronger than I was! I felt embarrassed as I watched them carrying my heavy bags.

Shun De: Country Garden School

The first weekend I was there I was asked to look after a dog for another teacher. He and his girlfriend had kindly taken me to the flower market so I could decorate my room, and they carried the heavy stone pots up the seven flights for me. So when I was asked to do a favour for them in return I did so gladly.

The only thing I didn't like about my new apartment was the Chinese toilet, or squatty potty as it was sometimes called. It was basically a hole in the floor with some tile around it. The local people believe this is much more sanitary than Western toilets with everyone putting their bums on the same seats. I think they have a point, but there's comfort to consider too. And it's much more comfortable to sit down if you have tummy troubles!

At the time you could still cross the river to the market on a small boat with a boatman pushing the boat with a pole. There was an old people's home on the other side, and we went to visit. Each person had their own room but shared a bathroom- with Western toilets! When I asked about this, I was told "It's because they can't squat any more. (I'm glad I'm not in China now, as I am now one of those "old" people.")

My Classes

Our students were from rich families, and every Friday afternoon there was a steady stream of Rolls-Royces, Lexus, and other expensive vehicles picking up the one child in the family. We foreign teachers wore jeans to class, and the Chinese teachers wore party dresses. Some of them greeted us on the way to class, but a lot of them ignored us.

I had a grade one class and a grade five class. The younger children were a lot better in English, and seemed to enjoy it a lot more. The students were badly behaved, though and I spent a lot of time "putting out fires." I think I needed some lessons in classroom management!

In the evening we got together at a very simple looking restaurant across a busy road. The tables were plywood but in spite of the modest décor, the food was delicious. We always invited Jeffrey, the liaison between the foreign teachers and the school. He translated for us, and we treated him to dinner. My favorite was spicy eggplant with lots of greens and beer in tall bottles.

We were not allowed to tip, even in fancy restaurants, because the Chinese feel they have to repay the favor, so we would "tip" them with our foreign postage stamps. They were delighted. No email in those days China had only been online for five years. . One thing we really appreciated was that they remembered what we liked. The coffee ice cream at one place was really good, and they would always offer it to me.

Another interesting thing about Chinese culture is that they are frugal with their finances. Sometimes this goes a little too far, and they miss out on things because they won't pay the asking price. We were at a fair, and the students were trying to bargain the price of a ride. The man wouldn't lower the price (which I thought was very reasonable) and they missed out. When a girl was shopping for vegetables for me (and bargaining), I ended up with wilted vegetables because she wouldn't pay the higher price.

Flag Raising Ceremony

Every morning the whole school assembled for the flag raising ceremony. The kids lined up in classes, and looked very sharp in their green and white uniforms. There were songs and speeches, and then all the students would march out in formation.

English Corner

This was an activity I had heard about but not seen, so I was anxious to find out what it was all about. It was a chance for the students to practice their English with a foreign teacher. They would surround the teacher and shout questions like, "Where are you from?" "Do you like Chinese food?" "Do you like Chinese people?" I used to say no to that one as a joke, but they didn't get it. This was a joke, but most of them didn't understand. I did really like my students, but not being treated as a deity. They did tend to treat us like royalty, which got a bit tiresome. I wanted to be treated just like an ordinary woman.

They would also ask:

"How old are you?' and "How much is your salary?" was also a common one but unusual in our culture. They say they do this so they know how to address people and how much respect to show them.

Home in Canada we usually find out these things by asking about their jobs and lifestyle.

Parks and universities all over China have English Corners, and one school I worked for had a different approach. They started a program called English Attack! and the students would shout English phrases, but not sentences: for example:

"I said to the man…!" It looked and sounded strange at 6 am on the sports field. They didn't get together to have real conversations but shouted into the air on their own.

Spring Festival – (Chinese New Year)

Another big part of Chinese culture is Spring Festival, which is actually held in mid to late winter, and it's a holiday for farmers to get together and relax with their families. It's the biggest holiday of the year, and EVERYONE travels home to see their loved ones. The holiday is now so big around the world that it's celebrated in many countries worldwide. Here in Canada there are many Chinese residents, so the festival is celebrated here. As I write we are just beginning the year of the rabbit, and I'm looking forward to some good Chinese cuisine.

I once took a train during that time, and there were hundreds, literally hundreds of people leaving the station. Some people had gone the wrong way and the guards were yelling at them. It was like being in a movie. I felt very uncomfortable being the only Western person there.

I was still in Guangzhou for Spring Festival in 1997 and it was a lonely one for me. This was before computers and cellphones. I had no books to read, no phone, and no teaching, so I spent a lot of time wandering the streets.

One day I ran into another foreign teacher who happened to have a large collection of John Grisham books which I happily devoured. What a relief to read books in English! I felt as if he had saved my life!

All the businesses were closed, but I had taken a pair of slacks to a dry cleaners', and went every day for two weeks to pick them up but the shop was closed. Finally after two weeks they were open again, but the man waved away my money when I tried to pay. This is another example of the kindness of the Chinese people.

Yangshuo

Li River

Guangzhou was a crowded, smoky city, and big trucks roared their way in and out of town spewing noxious fumes and belching smoke. The sky was yellow most of the time and the air was polluted. The Pearl River, where our fish came from, was polluted too, and it could be smelled from a block away. Guangzhou is situated on the Pearl River and I agreed with the article in the newspaper that bellowed, "The Pearl River-No Jewel!" The government spent twelve million dollars annually on cleaning it, but it didn't seem to make a difference. Even though I was living outside Guangzhou I would go into the city to teach in the evenings. I would have to breathe the noxious fumes on my way to class.

So, when I had a chance to get away for a short visit to "One of the most beautiful places in China," I jumped at the chance, and signed up to join two other girls to go to Yangshuo in the famous Guilin Province.

Yangshuo was a beautiful spot on the Li river, and the highlight of the trip for me was a boat trip on the river. Islands of all shapes, mostly finger-shaped pinnacles growing straight out of the water dotted the landscape. They are the famous Karst formations of which Halong Bay in Vietnam is one. The air was sweet and fresh and the scenery was a feast for the eyes.

One evening I went to watch the cormorant fishing in the evening, with the birds gorging themselves on as much fish as they could with a band around their necks. The fishermen got most of the fish this way, and someone said they thought it was cruel, but the birds still got a lot of fish for their effort.

Lots of vendors, with their wares on oxcarts, were everywhere, and it was fun bargaining as the prices went down every step we took farther away. I found a really nice jade magnifying glass and frog for my mother. This trip cost me a month's salary, but I would do it again in a minute!

Trip to Beijing: The Worst Night of my Life!

Every year the school would host a trip for the teachers to a different destination in China. The Chinese teachers had to have several years of seniority before they were allowed to go, but as a foreign teacher I was invited to go, and was very grateful for the opportunity.

There were five or six choices, all of which looked appealing, but Jeffrey wanted to go to Beijing, and as he was going to be my translator I agreed. We went by bus to the train station and then by train the rest of the way. There was no orderly line up to the bus. Everyone pushed and shoved their way on. When we arrived at the train station I saw all the Chinese teachers buying snacks in plastic packages. I didn't, because it was a 12- hour trip and I was hoping to get a real hot meal onboard. Big mistake! A man came around a bit later pushing an aluminum cart holding some tasty-looking chicken legs. I pointed to one, and enjoyed it. Tender and tasty. The Chinese people didn't buy any. None of them. Not even the children! (Photos of the train and the train attendant)

A few hours later, I climbed up onto my "hard sleeper," a bunk bed on the top row of three, and settled down for a good sleep. The rocking motion on a train usually lulls me to sleep, but not this time! It started out as a slight cramp, that developed into a roaring flood of pain and eruption. Every five minutes for the next few hours I had another attack, and I moved to a foldable seat on the bottom floor of the carriage so I could be ready for the next bout.

On the train, fold-up seats

The toilets, holes in the floor, were smelly and dirty, and it was very hard to balance with one hand as the train was moving fast. The swaying of the carriage and the eruptions in my stomach made it hard for me to stay on my feet. Whenever we stopped at a station the bathroom doors were locked, and once I banged on the door until the train staff opened it. I heard the word "foreigner." I must have woken up the whole carriage with the noise of my climbing up and down.

Finally, all the lights were turned on, and the man in the bunk below me, a doctor, gave me some little brown pills. The diarrhea stopped immediately and his wife gave me some clean baby-doll pajamas to wear. I don't know what I would have done without that couple. I was beyond embarrassment, as I was so ill, but I learned my lesson. "Don't buy food that other people are not eating!"

Beijing

As part of a tour group we were all dressed like children in green and white jackets, and carried backpacks. There were lots of other tour groups, and hordes of people around. It was easy to get lost.

Beijing was an amazing city, not only in size, (it is as large as the country of Belgium), but in attractions and we were fortunate enough to see the sights that many tourists see, including The Summer Palace, one of the most beautiful monuments in China, situated on beautiful Kunming Lake with its 17 arches.

We also visited The Forbidden Palace, where people were actually executed on the spot for approaching its wall. This went on for five centuries! It's now open to everyone, and its 9000 rooms cover 250 acres. (Jeffery and I got lost, not surprisingly, and had to get back to the hotel on our own!)

Jeffrey and me in a tuk-tuk

We visited the iconic Tiananmen Square, The Gate of Heavenly Peace- a misnomer, as this is the place where thousands of student protesters were massacred in 1989. One of my students told me he was there for the event, but didn't see any violence.

We found the prices cheaper than in Guangzhou, and we all bought souvenirs. Jeffery, a watermelon lover, showed up every day carrying a watermelon almost as big as he was.

The Great Wall

The last place we went to see was The Great Wall, which I was looking forward to, as it's the only manmade landmark visible from space, and stretches for 21,000 km (13,000 miles) from Liaoning near Beijing all the way across the mountains to the Gobi Desert. On the wall I found some postcard vendors, and as I was looking through a package of postcards to decide which ones to buy, along came Jeffrey, who snatched them and threw them on the table.

"What are you doing? You don't need those!"

One of the sellers grabbed him and threw him down on the cobbled stones, and his glasses went flying. One of our teachers, the tallest Chinese man I had ever seen, at about 6 feet 4, appeared a few minutes later and the man backed off.

We all kept walking and it was soon time to get on the bus. Everyone was there except for Jeffrey, and I kept looking at his empty seat next to me. Finally, a man got on the bus, said something in Chinese, and pointed to me. They wanted me to go somewhere. We went up a hill into a smoke-filled hut and there was Jeffery and the man from the Wall. I watched as one of the men from the wall walked over and handed him some money, and we left. He had gone to report the incident to the police, and they fined the men from the wall $60 and they also banned them from doing any more business up there. Jeffrey said he was satisfied with the result, and $60 would be a lot of money for him. His assertiveness paid off. Sixty dollars would be a fortune to him, as he had a very low salary.

Jeffrey and me

The Hong Kong Handover 1997

After our trip to Beijing this was the most meaningful trip a few months later. This was the year that Hong Kong would be handed back to China, after its 99-year lease to Britain. "One country, two systems" was to be the new form of government but now, 24 years later, it hasn't remained that way.

We had a few days' holiday for the special occasion and took the ferry to Lamma Island, one of the islands near Hong Kong with a very cheap hostel.

I arrived the day *after* the official handover to rainy skies. I met some fellow Canadians at the hostel and they invited me to join them to see the fireworks display from Victoria Peak., the highest point in Hong Kong. We took the double-decker bus, and my friends set up their tripods to photograph the event. They were well-prepared for the rain, and covered their cameras with little camera-shaped raincoats. Fireworks were invented in China, and the display was spectacular. (On Chinese New Year fireworks go off all night long, and nobody can sleep with the noise!)

I scanned the harbor for the royal yacht Britannia, but didn't see it. Someone told me later the yacht does not display its name for security reasons. But then I realized that the yacht had left with the former Governor, Chris Patton, the night before. A photo of his daughters crying was published in the paper the next day. Hong Kong had been their home for many years.

Photo of Mum and me

My Mother

After an interesting eight months in China, I decided to return to Canada to be near my mother, who had severe breathing problems due to her many years of smoking. At the time 70% of

Chinese men smoked cigarettes, and in Canada people would regularly smoke at their desks. My mother was one of them. She was an editor for The Vancouver Sun, and most of the people working there were smokers. This was a common practice.

By the time she decided to quit it was too late, and she only stopped when she was put on oxygen full time. She spent the last 10 years of her life breathing through a tube. When she first started using the oxygen she would joke about having a "New Leash on Life", but as time went on the oxygen became less and less effective. She would even have to choose between eating and breathing. She became painfully thin.

My Trip Home

Just after the Handover, I flew back in July from The Hong Kong airport. A long line of travellers snaked over to the check-in desk, and I had lots of bits and pieces of luggage scattered all over a space for about three people.

A helpful Chinese man kicked my things forward, looked at me for approval, and pushed them with his foot again as the line crawled forward. He did this until he had to change lines, and then he waved at me and motioned me to pick up my things. I was expecting to have to pay an overweight fee, but there were no problems at the check-- in, and they took everything with no extra charge.

My seat was the middle one in a section of five at the front of an enormous 747. A mother and her young daughter, a girl about eight or nine were sitting to my left. When the meal came the girl kept shaking her head but her mother force-fed her with a spoon until she threw up all over her tray table. Some mothers are very controlling.

We stopped in Taiwan to refuel, and then we were on our way to Vancouver. The captains were taking photos of the console and the pilots for the passengers. We passed our phones back and forth to the flight attendants, who took photos of the pilots and the cockpit, and passed them back to us. I got some really good photos.

Lost in Translation!

After landing in Vancouver, when we finally arrived at my mother's house she hugged me like she wasn't ever going to see me again! She had called the airlines, as the plane was delayed, and they told her there was a "problem" with the plane so we had to land in Taiwan. There was no problem, but it was windy and we had landed in Taiwan to take on fuel. Lost in translation!

Home in Canada- For a While!

I spent the next four years back in Canada, tutoring Asian students and, the last year, completing my TESOL Certificate. It was a six-month course with a practicum at the end, and I did mine at ISS (The Immigrant Services Society) in Vancouver.

I asked a Chinese friend to translate a one-inch by one-inch ad for tutoring in a Chinese newspaper. I charged $20 an hour, which I thought was reasonable. My first students were Sidney and Aileen, a brother and sister from Taiwan. I used to spend two hours at their place, tutoring one and then the other. (See photo of Sidney on the opposite page)

The first time I went to their house I was surprised to see the dad sitting on the couch in pajamas at 4 pm! He flew back and forth from Taipei to Vancouver every week. A lot of Asian businessmen did the same, as Asia is a better place to do business, and Canada has a better style of living. A newspaper article read, "Parenting by Fax" and that's how they did it. These days they would use Facetime or Zoom.

I enjoyed tutoring that brother and sister, with their year-round Christmas tree downstairs and their fluffy white Shitsu. But when I told them I was going to raise the price another five dollars an hour to $25.00 everything changed. They immediately returned all the teaching materials I had given them, and even the dog flapped his ears down in disapproval. They already had a math tutor and a music tutor, and I guess an extra five dollars wasn't in their budget. It was my last day, so I gathered up all my things and left.

Sidney and Aileen

Another student was Carman from Hong Kong, a social worker. She wore braces on her teeth and lived in a very small apartment. After a few months Carman returned to Hong Kong to care for her aging parents, and I was able to visit her there. She told me she wanted to meet a guy and get married, and I was really happy to see the wedding pictures on Facebook a few years later. She met Raymond at Toastmasters', a public speaking/social club. Luke, another student, was a ten-year-old boy from Taiwan. He was just delightful, and we both enjoyed the lessons.

He was very good at the paper art origami, and used to help his teacher with it, making animals and other interesting shapes.

Chapter 2

South Korea- 2000-2001.

Arrival in Seoul

A lot of schools and recruiters were advertising for schools in Korea, and they paid more than China, so I decided to apply and go overseas again. Let me clarify this was South Korea, North Korea did not hire teachers at that time. There were two or three schools interested in hiring me, but I liked the one with the recruiter Grace, who had a beautiful smile. I called her and told her I was going to go with another school because they were going to pay for my airfare. Immediately, she said they would pay, even though she had originally said they would not. So I started preparing to go overseas again.

I didn't realize she would later demand that I repay the airfare! After arrival she sent me an email threatening to cancel my visa and it turned out she wasn't so nice after all!

I sold all my furniture and got together with friends to say goodbye. A few days before the flight I started to feel very nauseous and head-achy, and if I hadn't sold my bed I probably would have stayed home for a few more days. David was kind enough to take me to the airport, and he suggested repacking my suitcase, but I wasn't up to it.

I didn't feel any better when I was finally onboard, but a nice flight attendant brought me some water and she even rubbed my stomach. In spite of her TLC however, a few hours into the flight my stomach felt queasy. I stumbled to the front of the plane to the bathroom, but only made it as far as the door. I was too sick to care.

When I got off the plane I felt a bit better. There was no sign with my name on it, but there was an information desk, and it was mid-afternoon, not the middle of the night like my first time overseas. The staff called my school, and I was told the woman who was coming to pick me up was stuck in traffic, a very common occurrence in Korea, and would be there as soon as she could. When she did arrive we headed out into a snowstorm. When we arrived at her place, one of the tall apartments, she left my bags in the car, and said they would be okay. I was going to stay in her home for a few days because of my health. They were so kind! They had rented the movie "The Gladiator" in English for me.

A couple of days later I was taken to my new apartment and to meet Heather, my new room-mate from New Zealand. She had left mid-summer back home, but said she didn't mind at all. She went off to take the subway as far as our school stop for a dry run. I wasn't ready for that yet. I didn't know my way around and I didn't know the money.

A day or so after I arrived I found a big plastic container under the sink.

"Oh good, dish soap!"

And I started on the dishes. Heather came in soon afterwards and asked me what I was doing. She informed me the plastic bottle was cooking oil!

I had a lot of trouble understanding her with her very strong New Zealand accent-pronouncing words like ear as air, and so on.

After a while she admitted that she spoke differently, but said, "It's only the vowels". One of the kindergarten kids told his mom she was pronouncing "egg" wrong. "Heather says it's "eeg!""

She also had a lot of different names for things, for example, she called a baseball cap a "beanie." I told her that she had the wrong words, and she got angry. I learned that people have different forms of English all over the world. It was okay to say beanie and also to say baseball cap.

She was very kind and went over my contract with me. It said nothing about repaying my airfare as long as I completed it. I completed a year there and it was enough for me, but If I had known I was going to have a traumatic experience I probably wouldn't have stayed for the full year.

We arrived in Korea in mid-winter, the same climate as Toronto, cold. snowy and windy. There was a statue of St. Venus de Milo outside and I used to joke that her arm had frozen and fallen off.

My First Day of Teaching: A Disaster!

The school didn't have central heating, and used small gas heaters to heat the classrooms. These heaters only lasted for a short time and had to be filled with gas. I had worn my new blue boots to stay as warm as possible as the hallways were freezing. They were made of the sort of nylon that looks good and is also warm.

Even inside the classrooms it was still cold compared to Canada, so I put the little heater as close to me as I could. A few minutes later, just as I was getting into the lesson, one of the girls interrupted me to call my attention to my boot, which was gradually melting! It was ruined. My new boots! My lesson was not to stand too close to a heater, as it could be dangerous.

McDonald's Meeting

A few days after I arrived I got a call at work from one of the students from my school in Gastown, who was back home in Korea visiting his family. I didn't teach him, but the whole school knew I was going to Korea after I posted a goodbye card on the bulletin board. The boy invited me to lunch, and we ate at a nearby McDonald's. He was using his mother's phone. I appreciated his kindness, And it was fun to see the Korean items on the menu in a "Western" restaurant. We sat on the third floor and discussed which of the girls passing down below he would like for a girlfriend.

Space Problems

Korea, a small country like Japan, also has a problem with space, and when I was dropped off the first morning I was surprised to see the parking garage. It's a big metal building with no doors. To use this, the driver stays outside, and punches in a code on a plate on a wall. After a lot of screeching and grinding noises a car-sized metal box appears and the driver drives the car into the box, and presses a code again. The car disappears, again with a lot of groaning and grinding noises. When the driver returns, the whole thing is done again, but in reverse order.

Another difference was the way people moved from one place to another. Because of the limited space, most people live in high rises, but they didn't use the elevators to transport their furniture and other things. They hire a giant crane with a flat bottom, and winch it up to the floor and the apartment where everything is unloaded onto the balcony. Some people don't bother, and leave their belongings out on the street and buy new.

I found a very nice orange couch one day that looked brand new, but by the time I convinced Heather to at least come and look at it, it was gone.

People replace their cars every two or three years and buy new. This was a big difference from China, but Korea is ten times wealthier.

Our Routine

We had two parts to our days: from ten to two we had the kindergarten, or the kindie kids, and when they went home at two I was ready to pack it in as well. It was an exhausting job with spoiled, crying children. We had 24 kids altogether, divided into groups. I bought a book to teach from, and when I left I donated it to the school. They liked the book and the curriculum I designed and used it for their own planning.

There were many kindergartens in Korea, in fierce competition with each other. In the early mornings the streets were full of mini-vans with cute pictures painted on them picking up children. The mothers were also super--competitive, and they would try to outdo each other with fancy cakes. We had a birthday party every Friday! The kids would line up and the teacher would use the same fork to feed cake to each child. It was a great opportunity to take photos with the teachers, especially those with a "foreign face". I am sure my photo is in a lot of albums with the little darlings.

After a break for a couple of hours, the middle school kids arrived. They had been in school all day, and didn't want to be there. They would run screaming down the hallways, as there was no playground. One of the doors was broken by the kids, but discipline was very lax because the school was running a business. As in many schools the business aspect was more important than the educational one.

We worked for a "hagwan," an after-school tutoring centre, and many of them were on a black list for teaching. Teachers were lied to, given their salaries late, and put into unacceptable housing. Our school was one of the better ones, but as I was doing research for this book I found it on the black list as well.

Heather had a friend from New Zealand, Tony. He pronounced it Tiny, even though he was about 6'4", who stayed with us for a while because his apartment was full of mould and his landlord didn't seem to care.

Heather was given the task of writing to new applicants from New Zealand. Most of the time she advised them not to come!

Sick Days

In Korea there are no sick days, and teachers have to teach even if they are at death's door. One day Heather was very sick, and stood up on the train all the way across town to the doctor, who told her to take a few days off and not to go to work until Monday. It was Thursday. As soon as she got home the school called her and told her to come in and teach. She told them what the doctor had said, and they told her to come in anyway because she was needed.

My Miserable Month of May

Two devastating events happened that month that I will never forget. The first one was the death of my mother, who, as I mentioned, hadn't been well for some time.

I was teaching my afternoon class one day and one of the girls from the office called me out of class. She said there was a phone call, "From your brother."

Oh, no! there was only one reason he would call me, if something had happened to my mum. I had called her about a week earlier, and I prayed to God to take her home to heaven as she was suffering so much. Her lung function test showed that she had "Very little lung function left," according to the doctor.

She had been living downstairs in my brother's house, to help with the mortgage, and someone was there all the time.

Gail, my sister-in-law, said she was upstairs resting and thought heard my mum call her.

"No, I didn't, Mum said, ''But I can't breathe, and I was wondering how to get your attention."

They took her to the hospital right away and she was squeezing my brother's hand, I think to comfort him more than her. While they were preparing a blood transfusion she stopped breathing. Gene and Gail were shocked when they learned she had passed away. They thought they would be bringing her back home with them.

After this devastating news from my brother I went back and tried to finish teaching my class, but I couldn't. I guess the news had affected me more than I thought. Heather was wonderful and volunteered to teach the class for me.

I flew back to Canada for the memorial – just a small party of family and a couple of her friends, as most of them were too old to travel. David picked me up at the airport, and I kept saying how happy I was to be back in Canada. All the flowers and trees were in full bloom. It was so good to be with family again, but I didn't want to stay and be without a job. There were lots of jobs overseas, but not in Canada, so

I flew back to Korea after only six days. My contract didn't finish until December, and it was only May, so I went back to finish the contract.

I hadn't cried, but I did on the plane on the way back, and wrote a short story about my mom, which ended up being published in the Globe and Mail under the category, "Lives Lived". I think it would have been better to approach the Vancouver Sun, where she was a writer and editor for many years, and more people knew her, but I wasn't allowed to publish in more than one place. My mother specialized in special interest stories.

She had a knack of getting people to open up to her, and people would tell her their life stories in coffee shops all over Vancouver. I once met a city counsellor she had written about and when I mentioned her name, Naomi Lang, she said, "Great Gal!" That was over 20 years ago now, and we still miss her.

Robbery and Rape!

I came back to a steamy, humid apartment in Korea, as the weather had suddenly turned hot in the few days I had been away, and the place was like a pressure cooker. I went shopping for a fan, found a second-hand one and lugged it home with me. It worked well, and I was just sitting down to enjoy the cool air when I heard a loud knock on the door. I looked out and saw a tall young man in an orange track suit. He was holding a piece of paper in his hand, and I thought he had brought me a bill to pay, as we had to pay our bills right at the door. He must have followed me home.

He said something to me in Korean, and when he could see I didn't understand, he drew a picture of a phone on a scrap of paper. I opened the door and let him in. Big mistake! I showed him the phone, and he used it, but then he called me over to speak to another man on the phone. I started to feel uncomfortable.

"Get out!" I screamed.

And that's when he pulled out the knife. It wasn't a large one, but I was frightened. He twisted my hands behind my back and found a piece of TV cable and tied them behind my back. It was really tight. He also blindfolded me, but before that, he said, "Sex?" I nodded because he had the knife. He carried me to a bed and He pulled my pants down.

Afterwards, he got up and started ransacking the apartment, and I prayed to God, "Save me!" I had seen his face, and thought he was going to come back and finish me off. I heard footsteps coming back! He said in my ear, "You shut up!" Then I heard his footsteps receding and the door open and close. He was gone! With the cable still binding my arms, I struggled to the door. One of the neighbours was just coming home, and I motioned him to help, but he just turned the other way. But another man came along and untied the uncomfortable cable around my wrists.

I hobbled over to my church, and explained what happened. The people were shocked and sympathetic, and drove me to a doctor in their van. But the doctor was not sympathetic at all. He examined me with a grim looking face. When I asked if he found anything in the examination he responded, "No special problem." I think he thought I was involved in a strange sexual cult!

The church members all prayed for me, and I felt their prayers. I only went for one counselling session, and the woman just told me all the ways I might feel in a similar situation. I was used to hiding my feelings, which is one way that people cope, and so that is what I did.

That same evening the phone rang. I was already in bed, and Heather answered. The person hung up. The phone rang again and Heather said it was for me.

I picked up the phone and heard, "You die!"

The man had stolen a ring from Heather, but she said it didn't matter because it didn't have any sentimental value. But I think the incident really affected her, and she was feeling depressed anyway. She sent an email to our boss (without telling me), asking if we could move to a safer place. The owners of the school also owned our apartment and we didn't have to move.

The next day I was invited to go to the police station and look through some photos. I found him right away, and the policeman said, "No, too far away." I thought there must be something wrong as he lived in Seoul, a 45-minute train ride from our place. They assured me they would catch the guy, but they finally admitted that they were not trying too hard as the penalty for rape was life imprisonment.

The only good thing that came out of this was the school owners gave us both cellphones. They got them in a special promotion, and didn't have to pay for them. It was good to have one.

The Church

I was very glad we didn't have to move because I had come to depend on my relationship with the church. It was only about 50 metres away, and I went there for the service every Sunday. The services were all in Korean, though, and my friend Yan translated it into English. It was a very poor translation, but I didn't have the heart to ask him to stop doing it because it must have taken him a long time.

I went to this church almost every week. The music was wonderful and one of the girls gave me a CD the choir had made. There was always a delicious lunch after the service and then choir practice. Most Koreans work six days a week and then spend Sundays in church. They like to keep busy, whereas we welcome our down time.

Soon after we arrived, Yan and one of the pastors from this church came to visit us in our apartment. Female underwear was hanging all over the furniture, and we laughed about it. Then, a few days later the same guys showed up carrying tools and a clothing rack, and installed it for us, still wearing their business suits. Such a kind gesture!

Sometimes I went to an English- speaking service downtown, but it was a long hot trip involving two trains. I did go to largest church in the world a couple of times. There were 10,000 people in attendance, and I thought it would be very impersonal. I was pleasantly surprised. I was escorted to an elevator, and then ushered to my seat in a balcony.

There were headphones for English translation and other languages. I even felt the presence of the Holy Spirit at that time!

We didn't work on Saturdays, so the director said the teachers didn't need a summer holiday because most Koreans worked six days a week and we had weekends off at our school. We explained the concept of an annual vacation, and that year, 2000-2001, was the first time the teachers were given a week off-at the end of July- the hottest week of the year. They were very excited and booked exotic vacations. One teacher even went to Europe.

Trip to Thailand; Koreans and Free Time

My friend Linda, who was teaching in another Korean city, wanted to go to Thailand for the holiday but the English-speaking travel agencies were fully booked. I asked Yan from church and he said he would try. He found us two tickets on a tour to Thailand in a Korean group. I enjoyed the holiday, especially after what I had just gone through, but the Koreans' itinerary was exhausting. I asked the tour organizers when we would have some free time just to swim in the pool or go shopping, but they said if there were no activities the Korean group members would complain and say they didn't get their moneys' worth.

Getting picked up in Thailand!

We were picked up by a baby elephant. When I went back to my class in Korea with my braided hair, one of the boys shouted, "Ugly hair!"

As I mentioned before, one aspect of Korean culture is that they don't like free time. This was true in other parts of their lives and the students were kept busy as well. All my students could play musical instruments, and they had tutors at home after their classes at school were over. A lot of them started school at 7 am and finished 12 hours later. They didn't mind the long hours if they were with their friends.

"Service"

One cold day I was trying to operate the coffee machine at the subway station. A man came along and showed me how to do it and handed me a coffee. When I tried to pay him, he said, "Service!" Another time I bought some makeup, and the lady put extra things in the bag. When I asked her about it, she said, "Service!"

And a woman with a meat store close to our apartment would come running out and give me free meat! Once it was raining and she came running with an umbrella! People seemed really anxious to be friendly and to help, especially foreigners. I liked that.

The Seafood Market

One day one of the Korean teachers asked me if I liked seafood.

"Yes! It's my favourite!"

I envisioned garlic prawns, Calimari and other delicacies. When we got to the market I saw a lot of live fish swimming in buckets waiting to be eaten. I was told to pick out what I wanted. Then I found out it was served RAW! They would serve squid in a broth, and told us it would wiggle as we swallowed it. Live fish like Jonah and the whale! Heather and I both said we would wait until it was cooked.

Aside from the seafood market the food was pretty good. The school would provide snack food from the stalls on the street, and we were welcome to graze on different noodle dishes and finger food between classes.

My favourite Korean food was Denchum chige. "Chige" means soup. It was a mildly spiced zucchini and chicken dish. Very tasty. I also liked Bibimbap, a rice dish with an egg on top. Delicious. I did try this here in Canada and the taste just didn't compare. Bulgogi, a sweetened beef dish, was another one of my favourites.

Kimchi

No mention of Korean food would be complete without its staple food, Kimchi. This is a Korean side dish of fermented vegetables that has been around for centuries. In the past there were no refrigerators, so fermentation kept the food edible. The dish contains fermented cabbage, garlic, spicy red sauce, onions, Korean radish, eggplant, beans, and sometimes meat. There are over 200 varieties of this food, according to the Kimchi Museum. This museum has kimchi-making classes, and a tasting room. Large pots that were used to store the sauce in the past circle the building, and a history of the dish, going back to Mongolia 2500 years ago is displayed on large panels in different languages.

Kimchi has a number of benefits for the health conscious. It's anti-aging. I met a Korean couple once and the woman told me she was 65. I thought she was about 40! It's also good for the immune system, and contains vitamins A, B, C, and K as well as amino acids.

Making kimchi at home is a social event, with a group of ladies getting together and mixing the dish with their hands. They wear rubber gloves because red sauce stains their hands.

No self-respecting Korean home is without a kimchi refrigerator. I used to tutor in Korean homes in Canada, and it would have a place of honor in the living room.

The red sauce in kimchi is called go chu sung. I would remember it as "Go chew the sun." I got used to it and would ask for it.

The Kimchi Explosion

Just before Christmas David and his girlfriend at the time, Laura, came for a visit. She was doing her PHD at SFU, and one of their friends, a Korean guy, asked them to bring back some kimchi for him, as it was much better in his home country. Before they left, David taped it securely in his backpack with duct tape, and when they got on the plane the pressurized cabin made it explode! There was kimchi everywhere, but they did manage to save some for their friend.

That backpack was very useful, and he carried it everywhere.

One night we were all invited to my friend Doae's place for dinner.

David was helping me with a plant, a gift for my hostess, and when we got off the first train, Laura said, "Dave, where's your backpack?"

It was on the overhead rack on the subway, and we all thought we would be able to retrieve it quickly. No such luck. We missed our dinner and visit with my friend.

We went to the ticket office and they said to go to the Lost and Found in the morning. David's passport, his airplane ticket, his Christmas gift from me, and his money were all inside. He and Laura went to the Lost and found early in the morning, confident that it would be there. I spent a lot of time praying.

They came back a few hours later, shoulders drooping, and said it wasn't there. They were supposed to fly to Japan that day, and Laura packed her things to leave. We were just about to take her to the airport alone when my cellphone rang. David was using it and he answered it. He listened, and joyfully asked, "You have my backpack?" You want to give it to me?" His smile got bigger and bigger!

The guy had seen the pack on the shelf by itself and took it home to look after it. He thought it might be stolen from the rack if it stayed there. We met him a few hours later, and he wouldn't take any money or even go for a coffee with us. This meeting made David late getting to the airport, but they were bumped up to first class for the short flight.

Heather didn't seem to want to hang out with me, and said she felt more comfortable with her friends from New Zealand. I found out that *The Korean Herald* put personal ads in the paper for free, and so I advertised for new friends. So many responses! Every time I opened my email I found at least 25 new ones.

Han Pilyeo and her husband

Dinner at Han Pilyeo's house

One was from Rhonda, a Canadian woman from Victoria, and one morning I gave her a call before work. She was staying with a Korean family and the tv was on. She said there was something happening in the US, but the broadcast was all in Korean, and she didn't know what was going on. Her landlady finally came in the room and told her. There was an attack on the World Trade Centre in New York!

What a shock! There's a big US army base in Seoul, so there was reason to be concerned. We joined the entire Western World in its grief. Heather's sister lived in New York and Heather said she complained about the smoke for a long time afterwards. It must have been terrible living in a place that looked like a war zone, and in a sense it was. Television sets all over the world broadcast scenes of smoke and devastation at the World Trade Centre site.

However, our students, middle school and younger, liked Osama Bin Laden, and would come to class wearing hoodies. They pranced around the classrooms acting like terrorists. Did they think it was all a video game?

When I went home a few months later guards outside the airport were all brandishing Kaleshnekovs.

Sand Sculpture: Busan South Korea

Chapter 3

Northern China. Chifeng, Inner Mongolia

I spent the next few months teaching in Canada, but was unable to secure full time employment. Again, there was a plethora of jobs overseas. I wasn't very keen on going back to Korea, though I met some lovely people there, and an ad for a teacher in Inner Mongolia caught my eye. It was only a 4-month contract.

I thought: "I can do this!"

After a couple of emails and interviews I was hired for the job in Inner Mongolia in Northern China. The young man and his fiancée who interviewed me were from China and were living and working in Vancouver. He was the son of my new boss: Mr. Hao. "Hao" means "Good." in Chinese, and I was hoping he would be. The salary was good, at $2000 USD a month with free accommodation. Maybe I would be able to save some money.

They gave me a suitcase, and a Notebook (computer) to take with me and gave me a ride to the airport. When we landed in Beijing, there it was! - big sign with my name on it! A group of six people had come to meet me, teachers and school officials, and we travelled the five hours by mini-van. It was good to be back in China and see its three- wheeled tractors, that I hadn't seen anywhere else. We stopped for a delicious meal on the way.

One of the men who came to meet me was a teacher and also an artist. On the landing on my way up to the fifth floor there was an incredibly beautiful painting of The Great Wall that he had painted. I thought it should have been in an art gallery.

I was given a beautiful apartment on the second floor of a building. The lower floor was Mr. Hao's office, and a bedroom for the three girls who were "looking after me." They took turns sleeping in that room, and I was never alone. (I found out later that they were not just being nice; if anything happened to me, such as a rape, the school would lose face in a big way.)

One day, towards the end of the term, we were all invited to a fancy lunch at a restaurant. I was working on my BA and had planned to use the day to study, so I said I didn't want to go. The girl with me that day said, "If you don't go, then I can't go." So we went, and toasted and feasted for 3 hours. After all that toasting I was ready for a nap, and I really enjoyed the food, especially the steamed fish!

My First Day

I only had 2 classes initially, a grade five class in the early morning and one in the evening, a conversation class with teenagers. I gave them a prompt- We went to the hospital- and one boy finished it "To "Off"" the baby! I was expecting something innocuous like "To visit my grandmother."

I enjoyed Chifeng, but it wasn't a tourist destination. When I arrived there I looked everywhere for postcards to send home. Nobody had them. Chifeng is famous for its dumplings though, and we went to a place that had 40 different kinds of them! They had never seen a foreigner before, and they gave me a free lunch, and beer!

We travelled there by taxi, as this was before Uber, etc. and my favorite driver was a heavy man. I called him the "fat taxi driver" and so did the other people. Later on I would see him sitting in his taxi looking miserable while other drivers were having lunch. He said he was trying to lose weight.

There were some forests nearby with the trees all standing in strict lines like the PLA (People's Liberation Army) soldiers. They must have been planted during the Cultural Revolution in the 1970's.

The Chinese and Relationships
Trip to Beijing

One day, one of the girls told me we were all going to Beijing to buy books, and I could choose the ones I wanted for my class. On arrival we finally found the area where the books were sold, and I was about to start browsing when one of the men got a call on his cellphone. We had to leave and go to another store, because somebody knew the owner there. In China it's all about relationships.

Chest Pain

This group culture of relationships was again revealed to me when I got sick a few weeks later and had to visit the hospital.

I felt a pain in my chest as I was climbing the stairs to my classroom on the fifth floor. As soon as I passed the third floor the discomfort began.

They did an x-ray, but Tina forgot the English for "Take a deep breath". I figured it out.

Next, we went to a hospital. I was not impressed. It was old, cold and dirty.

"Don't touch anything," said Tina, as I passed doorways with piles of garbage in front of them. In spite of the chilly wind there was no front door to the hospital, only a heavy tarpaulin in the doorway.

"Isn't there another hospital in the city?" I asked.

"Yes, a brand new one, but Mr. Hao's sister-in-law works **here!"**

It turned out I didn't have heart problems, and they did some other tests but decided that my discomfort was from an infection in the muscles of my chest. (In Canada and got exactly the same diagnosis.)

Mrs. Hao

Mr. Hao's wife lived in Beijing, and she took over my care, grabbing my hand to cross the busy streets. Like many Chinese couples they didn't live together, as many of them relocate for work and only see each other a few times a year. Theirs was an arranged marriage, which was common at the time, but they seemed very happy.

Mr. Bean

After a month of physio I was feeling better and returned to class. I was given a lot of classes, but they were only once a week. I decided to make it fun for them by showing Mr. Bean videos and teaching a few words in English every class. It was fun and we all enjoyed him and his crazy antics.

Getting Colder

The Moon Festival in October started the cool season. It's customary to sit outside and look at the moon, but it was too chilly for me and I was only able to sit outside shivering for a few minutes.

It was warm inside the school, but the students had to run around the field for an hour every morning for exercise, and were only excused if they were sick. I visited one of the boys in the hospital, and he had the customary drip in his arm. The Chinese use this IV treatment for a lot of illnesses, and even used it on me when I had stomach problems.

North vs South

The north of China is different from the south. The people are taller in the north, and when I asked I was told it was because their diet was based on wheat and not on rice, as in the south.

I used to go on shopping trips to the town, and after paying I would look around for my purchases. They were gone, carried by my students, or whoever I was with. They would report to Mr. Hao what I had bought. The Chinese are very curious people!

Mr. Hao bought me a gift, a big water tank with fish inside. The aquarium didn't have a pump, so I was forever washing and cleaning it. I gave it back to him, and he got me some birds to replace them. He then bought a pump and a light for the aquarium.

The Grasslands

We took a trip to the famous Grasslands, but the grass wasn't there. It was like going to La Conner in Washington State, to see the tulips and seeing brown fields.

In spite of it being the wrong season to see the grasses, it was great being in the wide-open spaces, and sleeping in a yurt.

They gave us rancid tea with butter in it and tough beef. I thought this was going to be our dinner, but they were just giving us a sample of what the herdsmen used to eat. They gave us some tasty food later on. Some of the boys in our group rode the horses.

The Cold

The school itself was very warm, but not my apartment. I bought a very thick quilt for my bed, and asked for a space heater for my bedroom. There was a heater the other end of the apartment, but it was grounded to the wall and couldn't be moved.

"No! They are dangerous!" was the answer to my request, but I was finally given a cheap one. It was completely useless, and heated the area above it for about one inch! I would try to warm my hands by putting them almost on top of it.

There were nights when I would lie in bed needing to go to the bathroom. I would put it off until I couldn't wait any longer, then make a mad dash to the bathroom.

For bathing, I would quickly strip to have a shower, and then put on all the layers of clothing I needed to keep warm. First, long underwear, and socks, then pyjamas, then a dressing gown. Then another mad dash back to bed.

I didn't have a clothes dryer. The Chinese don't use them, which is good for the environment but not very convenient. So my wet clothes were draped over the shower and the toilet whenever I did the laundry, and I had to move them to use the bathroom.

But at least I had a washing machine. I went to visit the students' dorm, and saw one girl sitting on the floor scrubbing clothes in a bucket!

My Best New Year's Eve

I was in Chifeng for New Year's Eve, and was surprised by how much fun it was. The students had moved all the desks to the perimeter of the classroom and one wall was left empty for the performers.

They had decorated with paint and streamers and everyone was in a happy mood. The floor was littered with orange peels, candy wrappers and sunflower seed shells.

One by one, the students would come and perform. Some of them played Chinese instruments, and some sang or read poetry. It was a lot of fun, and I spent my time visiting all the classrooms and enjoying the entertainment. I was treated like an honored guest, but, thinking back, it might have been a good idea for me to have prepared my own presentation.

My Gift

One day I decided to buy a new bra. We went downtown, and ran into the mother of one of my students. She wanted me to "do something for him," and said she wanted to buy me a gift. I tried to explain that the marks had already been submitted.

When she saw my old bra she threw it across the street! We all had a good laugh.

She insisted on paying for a new one and and a warm pair of pyjamas as well; and when I saw the huge roll of money she pulled out I stopped protesting.

I asked if I could extend my contract, as I had no job in Canada, but I was told the new principal "Isn't even paying the Chinese teachers."

Leaving Chifeng

I had joined the school just as the nice principal was retiring, and the new principal didn't have the same empathy.

So I left again, sorry to say goodbye to the three girls who had been looking after me who had become friends. One of them gave my birds to her auntie.

The day I left I called Mr. Leong, the man who had painted The Great Wall to say goodbye. Half an hour later we were enjoying delicious food. They had an impromptu going away party for me!

Just recently, I looked up Chifeng to see how it is now. A video by a German guy who was at the train station. Freezing! Some things don't change. I left by this same station, and I was warned not to leave my bags unattended, as it was a place known for robberies. We saw one young man looking at my bags with great interest.

One of the students, "Peter," came from a rich family. His parents owned factories, and he had six siblings, during the time of the "One child policy." The laws didn't apply to the wealthy.

His parents had an apartment in Beijing, and invited all of us to stay there for a few days. His mother had had bunk beds installed to accommodate everyone. There were seven of us.

I thought the heating was just fine, with no drafts, but one of the girls said it was "Too hot."

Shanghai

David was coming for a visit at the end of my contract, and we picked him up in Beijing. The airline and the flight number were different, but we managed to find him on the only foreign plane. Peter's family had a driver, and this made it easier.

He spent most of his time working on his Chinese, and bought a tape player to listen to the language. We did some sightseeing around Beijing, and then got ready to board the train for Shanghai. I had prepared an itinerary to visit Shanghai and Hainan, a tropical island in the south. After my disastrous experience the first time on a Chinese train, I didn't expect much, but this time I was amazed! It was a fast train, very clean and comfortable. There were not only Western toilets, with sit down seats, but they were made of oak! State of the art!

In Shanghai we stayed at a heritage hotel, now used as a hostel. Men stayed separate from the women, and this suited me fine because I am an early riser and David is not. Some famous people stayed in this hotel in the past. One of them was Charlie Chapman, and there were other famous guests from that era. I think Clark Gable was one of them.

The floors were polished wood, and the room I was in was clean and comfortable with everyone in their own cots. I befriended a Japanese lady who was very kind, but she left after a couple of days for the "Panorama" – the view from one of the nearby skyscraper hotels.

Our hostel was close to the "Bund", a famous seaside walking place, full of local people taking photos, repairing shoes, and providing other services for foreign tourists. David's shoes were not in good shape; the sole was coming off one of them. He gave it to a man, who immediately took the entire shoe apart! He did a good job repairing it, but didn't ask if he could do this.

(A similar thing happened to me in Nanning, where a woman took my shoes apart and then asked me for a huge amount of money. There was a crowd of about 20 people surrounding me, and I gave the woman what I thought it was worth and then went back to my school. They told me that I had done exactly the right thing.)

Our next destination on our mini-tour was Hainan Island, officially known as Hainan Dao, in Chinese. Hainan, the name of the island

and the province, means "South of the sea," and it is the largest and most populous island in China. We flew there from the mainland-a short one hour flight.

A driver from our guest house met us at Sanya airport, and took us to a hostel close to the beach. For us, coming from Beijing, and winter, this was an island paradise, and it was hard to believe it was January, as we swam in the warm waters, ate juicy sweet mangoes sold to us by local ladies, and bought summer clothing to relax in. I wanted to go back again to the warm seas and delicious seafood! We spent a few days enjoying the sun and the sand, then it was time to return to Canada and to winter.

Chapter 4

Nanning, Vietnam and Beihai

I didn't stay long in Canada. Jobs were scarce, and again, there were lots of jobs overseas.

My next destination was Nanning, known to be the friendliest city in China. I did find the city very friendly, especially to foreigners. But not everyone appreciated this.

One teacher I met told me she was reading her book on the bus, and a Chinese man sat beside her and said, "I want to practice my English."

"Well, I don't!" was her reply and that was that. Sometimes it's fun to escape into a good book when the foreign experience gets to be too much!

Nanning is known as "Green City", with over 2000 varieties of evergreens and fragrant flowers. The highways are lined with vegetation, to protect the environment. A water truck refreshes these plants every day, with a person sitting on top of the truck and hand watering the trees, flowers and other foliage along the roadside. This also keeps the dust from the road down.

This city is the political, economic and cultural centre of Guangxi Province, and people driving down the wide University Blvd. are greeted with a large billboard with photos of the "Great leaders"- Mao Tse Tung, Deng Xiao Ping and Jiang Xiamen.

This province borders on Vietnam, and I was able to take a short trip there, on a city bus to the border, and then a mini-van to Vietnam.

It took a long time to get there, because one of the guys kept yelling at people to get on the van. It was very annoying.

We travelled all night, and I was the only woman onboard. I desperately needed to use the bathroom, and they didn't want to stop. I finally convinced them and they stopped on the side of the road next to an embankment. I climbed up there and there was nothing around but a house, and I ended up using their backyard lawn for my business, with the van blasting its horn. Luckily it was very early in the morning and the people weren't up yet!

Spring Festival Trip to Beihai

Our Spring Festival holiday was coming up and I wanted to return to Hainan Island and its beautiful beaches. Ferries sailed there from the city of Beihai, and my plan was to go for a few days holiday. Someone at work gave me the address and phone number of a good hotel, so off I went.

I found the hotel, but it seemed awfully quiet. The man behind the desk said that I could have a room at the hotel, but the ferries were not running because of the holiday. Oh no!

He was the manager, and said he wanted to invite me for Chinese New Year dinner at his house. How kind is that!

He said he would pick me up to take me to his home at 4 pm. He didn't come, and I thought, "Oh well."

But half an hour later there he was at my door. His home was full of family members, and most of them could speak English. The food was incredibly aromatic and delicious. (A lot of Chinese women start cooking this special meal at three am!) I had a great time, and when the manager dropped me off, he said breakfast would be delivered to my room in the morning, and after that a car would come and take me sight-seeing!

We had a wonderful day, with some of the girls wanting to practice their English, and taking in the sights of the city. A couple in the van with their young son invited me to their home to have dinner and to watch the fireworks. The illuminations and explosions were spectacular, sponsored by the Bank of China.

Gunpowder was invented in China over 2000 years ago, and fireworks were invented when a Chinese monk from Hunan Province put gunpowder in a bamboo tube and blew on it. The loud noise is meant to keep evil spirits away. Anyone trying to sleep during Chinese New Year will attest to this!

There is a sequel to this story. A couple of years later Bob and Patty, American friends, arranged a trip to Beihai. I went with them and some Chinese friends of theirs, and wanted to look up the same hotel and the same lovely man, if he was still working there. Luckily I had kept the name card (business card) of the hotel, and we took a taxi. He was there! He immediately got on the phone as before, and a few minutes later, the mini-van arrived, and the same people as before, and we spent another wonderful day together. I had a lifelong memory of the kindness of the Chinese people.

I worked for three different schools in Nanning, the first one being AV – for Audio-Visual. The students were all ages, from elementary to business clients, which I preferred. I became friends with Joanna, another Canadian, and Vincent, a charming Chinese teacher. I shared a flat with Joanna for a while, and she was into foot massage. Sometimes we went twice a week. My feet had never felt better.

Vincent and his young daughter Susan lived in an apartment on Nanhu Lake, and I enjoyed visiting them. People ran, skated, and biked around this lovely park.

Special events were held there, and one memorable night I took Susan to the Lantern Festival. We floated our little candle in its paper boat, along with hundreds of others in the moonlight.

After Joanna became a manager we didn't get along as well, and she said I hadn't completed my task satisfactorily. I was teaching a class for another teacher, and they wanted me to write the topics studied, and I just wrote the page numbers. I was suddenly out of a job.

I sat down and googled, "Teach Nanning," and I applied for the first job that came up. It was the first vocational school in Nanning, and had been there for a long time. They needed English conversation teachers. The job was very easy, and the only problem was there were some students who were very eager, and tended to dominate the class, and some who sat in the back sleeping. Chinese students always find English names for themselves, and I had one class with "Back," "Middle", "Peach", "Apple", "Summer" and "Winter" as my students.

This made it a lot easier for the foreign teachers, as Chinese names are in three parts, and it's a lot to remember. Each class had a class monitor and they were a big help because the average class size was fifty.

The money wasn't great, but there was free accommodation. Buses were only two yuan, but they broke down frequently. I got to know if a bus was parked near our school it was broken down. Our bus was "222" or in Chinese, "RRR!"

The Hot Badminton Player

Female Chinese teachers were forced to retire at 50, and one of these women anxiously waited in the parking lot for the teachers' bus every day with her badminton racquet in her hand. She was the strongest player, and could have handled a class easily. I found the Chinese very ageist in their thinking.

The arriving teachers would have a brisk game of badminton every evening before dinner, and this lady was the best player! They played every day, even on the very hot days, and they even let me play sometimes.

Power Cuts

There were often power cuts. I soon realized that they happened just when we were going to break for lunch, and would go back to my apartment to no air conditioning and no cooking. I couldn't even make a cup of tea. I would phone a friend in another part of town, and ask if they would like a visit. The answer was always, "Yes", and I would get on a bus and go and visit them for an hour or two. We found out that Nanning was selling its power, and it was very inconvenient for us.

One time we were all set to watch a performance, and the power went off in front of the whole school. We were all sitting outside on little wooden stools waiting for the show to begin, and one of the teachers, Brent, started a chant: "Turn on the power! until someone found a generator.

We had congenial colleagues. Brent and Trina, from New Zealand, were very friendly, and Brent would call in the evening to see how my classes had gone.

Another New Zealander, Catherine, was a 29- year- old farm girl, and her parents came to visit her. They didn't mind the spartan accommodations at all. Catherine went home to buy her own farm, and also to become a police woman.

(Photo of Trina and Chinese woman with special needs)

All Foreigners Look Alike

Justine was a young woman from Canada who joined us, and she had to go back to Canada for her grandmother's funeral. She was a few days late returning to Nanning, as she was there for Canada's National Day on July 1, Canada Day when all the government offices were closed, so she had to wait a few days to get her visa back to China.

One of the senior teachers from the school saw Catherine one day before class and lit into her, saying, "Your students are waiting for you!"

Catherine, who was 10 years older than Justine, had auburn hair, and Justine had blonde. This was not appreciated by Catherine!

Catherine was friends with Cindy, a Chinese English teacher. She was fun to be with and Catherine's family wanted to sponsor her to study in New Zealand. The Chinese government refused, and said they didn't know if she would come back again. I tried to contact them and put in a good word for her, but it was no use.

I didn't understand their thinking. If a country as overcrowded as China loses a few people to emigration, why stop them? Control issues? I heard that only three percent of the emigrees return.

A few months after I started working at the college they told me that they had an opening for a teacher. Maybe my son would like to apply? They said afterwards they liked the idea of family members working together.

David and I at the Same School

He did come, and did end up staying in China for ten years! He eventually became fluent in Cantonese and Mandarin. I was very impressed when he picked me up in Hong Kong on a visit, and started asking questions about where to pick up luggage. The man didn't understand his Mandarin, and he switched to Cantonese. Very impressive. He says he isn't fluent, but he sounds fluent to me.

Our working together only lasted for one semester. I had some health issues, and David had a problem with a class, so our contracts were not renewed. It was good to see him there though.

The Endoscopy

It was very hot and humid in Nanning and I was drinking a lot of coke. I would often ask a student to get one for me and one for themselves. One night, while I was out having dinner, I took a sip of wine and got a really sharp pain in my belly. I went to the doctor, and he told me they would give me some medicine to clear it up, and if that didn't work they would have to do an endoscopy.

In this procedure they put a cable down your throat into your stomach, and a little camera on the end takes pictures of everything down there. It didn't sound like fun. To begin with I had to fast for 12 hours, and then another hour after the procedure, as it might cause irritation.

Seeing a doctor is very cheap in China. The hospital where all the doctors worked was right next door to our college, and we only had to pay two yuan to see a doctor. It was four yuan to see a specialist. Five yuan was equal to one US dollar.

Well, the meds didn't work so I had to have the endoscopy. The whole procedure only took about five minutes, but it seemed longer. I gagged when they put the cable down my throat, and then they taped it in place around my mouth. I had to remain perfectly still.

"Very interesting, mom!" David said. They did find a small ulcer, and so I was off alcohol, spicy food, coca cola and greasy food. It cleared up.

A very pretty Chinese doctor was called in to translate for us. Her name was Rachel, and she came to a party I had the next weekend. David's friend Julian was there too, and they became an item. I was surprised because he's a heavy smoker and she's a doctor. She didn't seem to mind the smoking, and they have been happily married for years now. They took me out for a drink the last time I was in Nanning.

Nanning is in the far south of the country, but it does get as cold as Vancouver for about six weeks every year. People wear their winter clothes inside. Once I was invited to a birthday party. One of the foreign teachers had adopted a little girl, and everyone brought her warm clothes as birthday gifts.

Most of the year, though, Nanning had a warm, tropical climate, and we wore our summer clothes. It had a very good tailor's market, and I had some clothes made there. One, a blouse, I still wear, 17 years later. Clothes were just too small in the stores.

Nanning had a Mcdonald's, and it was the only restaurant that was heated. It was packed. I used to go there to use the Western toilet upstairs.

One day I saw some Chinese men ordering children's meals and laughing about it. There were no kids at their table.

My last year in Nanning.

I was hired at the Guangxi International College of Technology, Nanning Branch. It happened this way. I was researching the different schools around town, and people said the Science College was a good one, but there was litter all over the school grounds, and this bothered me.

My college was in the north of the city, a little bit out of the way, but it was clean. They showed me the teacher's apartment, and there was a bathtub!

"Oh, you have a bathtub!" I cried in delight, and the girl showing me around said,

"Are you going to make your decision now?"

I did soon after.

The students at this college were more serious than the ones at my former school, and my accommodation was better.

The Floods

In the rainy season in Nanning the water would run in torrents down the street. David, who was employed at the Shipping School, came to visit me, and he was inching along the ledge outside of the gate to the school, and put his hand on a sharp spike on the top of it. Ouch!

Once I was on a bus and we were stuck on a flooded street. Traffic was backed up. The men chuckled as they took out their cellphones. I would say the attitude of the Chinese is "Don't sweat the small stuff." Not surprisingly, there is no road rage in China!

I stayed at this school for almost a full academic year. I was planning to complete my contract, but I got an email invitation to my daughter's wedding. I was the birth mother, and she already had a wonderful mom, so I was honored to be invited.

We had met through an ad in the paper. You know, the ones that read, "Happy Birthday, female adoptee born on … in …."

It was an exciting day for both of us. I met her on her nineteenth birthday.

I had a pretty Chinese dress (qipao) made for the wedding. This was a long dress with a slit up the side, with flowers and birds embroidered on one side and with a little jacket to match. It was a beautiful turquoise colour, and the whole outfit cost $15 for the materials and sewing. It was beautifully made with no loose threads and I wore it for years.

I asked to be released from my contract a week early, and after a lot of discussion back and forth I was told I could go. The school paid my airfare back to Canada, but one of the teachers told me it was only because the school officials didn't understand the HR person, or something like that. (They were all speaking Chinese, but the local dialects differ a lot).

My Trip Home

The flight home had a stopover Hong Kong, and I experienced the famous "Chungking Mansion." It is written up in the guidebooks as a cheap place to stay. It was cheap, but looked like a haunted house in a horror movie. My room was so small I could barely fit my suitcase inside, and the blue carpet got soaked when I took a shower.

The hotel was in a great shopping area though, and I found a beautiful hand-made embroidered tablecloth for the happy couple. I also bought some beautiful white silk pyjamas while I was on a tour of the harbor. The Chinese are very enterprising salespeople and go after tourists and their money wherever they may be. Goods for sale were under my seat on the boat, so I didn't have far to go. I love the satiny feel of silk next to my skin.

After two days of travelling, I arrived in Victoria, B.C. where the wedding would be held. Val, the bride, had arrived after a manicure, and I thought to myself how alike we are in many ways. Neither one of us likes long nails or nail polish.

The wedding was held on a glorious spring day, one of the "dazzlers" as my mum used to call them. The bride arrived by boat at their home on the Gorge Waterway. A friend of hers, Jamie, a former boyfriend, was her "Best Man." She was wearing a lacy, heritage style dress and she looked very beautiful.

I stayed in Victoria for two months, working at a language school downtown and researching jobs in the Middle East. I was focused on that part of the world because the money was better and I wanted to teach a totally different language group.

Chapter 5

Seven Years in Oman

Photo Credit Unsplash

An Easy Decision

I wanted to secure a teaching position by September or October, because most of the ESL Schools would close when the Koreans and Japanese students returned home to their universities.

I applied to Nizwa University in Oman. Most people have never heard of this country, or confuse it with Amman.

"That's in Jordan, isn't it?"

The reason a lot of people haven't heard of Oman is that it was basically closed to other countries until the 1970's, when the last Sultan took over. His goal was to modernize the country, which meant building a lot of roads and schools, and getting the Bedouin boys out of the desert and into school. Before his time, there were only a couple of main roads and one hospital for the whole country.

I had also applied to Guangxi University in Nanning, my last posting in China, which had a very good reputation, but they wanted me to pay my own airfare plus $1500 US to work there! This money would be returned at the end of the contract. I think they must have been cheated by other teachers who don't always act with integrity in foreign countries.

It wasn't a hard decision. When I asked if the school in Oman would pay my airfare I was told, "No problem."

I stayed with my friend Marge in Richmond, and she insisted on taking me to the airport at three am!

Arrival in Oman: Man in My Room!

When I arrived in Muscat, the capital, a couple of days later, a man wearing a white robe and a warm welcoming smile picked me up and took me to a luxury hotel where I spent the next few days.

I noticed there was a spa on the top floor, so went up there for a massage. It felt great-just the thing for a weary traveller. The masseur told me I had to pay downstairs at the desk, so I took the elevator downstairs to the lobby with him. I hardly noticed the man behind the desk, but he must have noticed me, because about five minutes later, there was a loud knocking on the door, and the same desk clerk was standing there. I asked him what he wanted.

He said, "I'm sorry. I'm sorry."

"Yes?"

Then he said, "You had a massage."

"Right."

"Did it feel good?"

"Yes. And?"

I let him know that my massage had nothing to do with him, and he left. This was the first time that an Arab man behaved inappropriately, but not the last.

I found out later on that the thinking is that "Western women are easy." We blamed the media. A lot of the TV stations are Western-based with soap operas, game shows and other non-Islamic programming.

The Majan Guest House.

After a few days at that hotel we were taken in a mini-van to Nizwa, where our university was located. It was a two-hour drive, and I enjoyed looking at the desert scenery. A lot of it was rocky, which surprised me. The few trees had clusters of goats huddled under them. It was very hot out there, and they knew where to find shade.

We stayed at the Majan Guest House for six weeks until our apartments were ready. They cleaned our rooms for us every day and the Indian staff were friendly and helpful.

One strange thing I noticed was a large arrow on a paper glued to the bedside table. A small rug was in this table. I then realized that the arrow was the direction of Mecca, where all Muslims have to face when they are praying, and the rug was a prayer mat.

One afternoon, Sue, a Canadian teacher in her second year at Nizwa University, brought mats and food over for us new teachers. We had a picnic in the small park and got to know each other sitting on the grass. We didn't have cooking facilities and the hotel food was limited, so her kindness was greatly appreciated.

The University was in Birkat-al-Mouz village, (banana village in English) and Nizwa was very small at that time. There was only one supermarket, Lulu's, and its air-conditioned aisles were a good place to get out of the heat.

Toilet Paper

One morning a woman from the office got on our bus, and said she was collecting one Rial ($2.50) from each teacher for toilet paper, as Omanis didn't use it. We all paid except one teacher, who refused on principle. The Omanis use water guns to spray themselves. This works well except when the water is cut off.

Students' Dress

The first time I saw a group of Omani students I was shocked. Most of our students were girls, and were covered in black from head to toe. Seeing 20 girls dressed like this was unusual for me, but I soon got used to it. Sometimes we teachers would take a peek at their hair when they were rearranging their scarves in the ladies' room, and it was flattened by their scarves. They told me they only have a haircut once a year.

Their abayas had long sleeves and were loose fitting, so the form of the women couldn't be seen. One of the teachers said they could still convey their sexuality by the way they walked.

Everything was covered but their faces, and some of them were veiled. Thank God we teachers didn't have to cover, but we did have to wear long sleeved tops and long pants or skirts. One day I was having lunch, and when I was cutting my chicken with its bright red sauce it splattered all over my white top. There wasn't time to go home and change so I quickly scrubbed off the stain under a tap. The wet cotton stuck to my body, and my loose top was suddenly form-fitting. One of the Omani teachers complained about me.

The boys wore their long white dishdashas to school, with turbans and/or caps on their heads. Sometimes I would see them in town and I wouldn't recognize them in their t-shirts and shorts. "Hello, Teacher!" I used to hear this and stare at those students. They would have to remind me who they were because they looked so different.

The girls didn't have the same freedom, and were locked up in hostels with short trips on a bus to buy candy.

Once I said, "Have a nice weekend" to the girls, and one of them said, "In the hostel?"

My First Class

The first week I asked the students what they liked to do in their spare time. Listening to music was a popular pastime in China, but, apparently not in Oman.

When asked if they liked listening to music, the students answered, "Oh no, teacher, only the Holy Koran."

I found out this wasn't entirely true. A few months later we were all invited to a wedding, and the girls danced and sang along to all the top hits. They knew all the words! In Oman often the truth would be buried in the shifting desert sands.

The students in China loved to take photos everywhere, but not my students in Oman. It was okay to photograph the boys but not the girls. Even in weddings there are no photos of the bride, "In case a man looked at them."

We were allowed to take photos of one bride, however, a beautiful girl who worked in the office, but we had to promise not to show them to any men.

I thought it would be fun for the students to communicate with my Chinese students as pen pals, but there wasn't enough interest. Most of the students had little knowledge or interest in the outside world. They knew about the Sultan, who they adored, and Sadam Hussein, who one wrote was a "nice man."

Gender Disparity

Sometimes the female students would do presentations in front of the class, and it was one activity they really enjoyed. The boys, however, would stand at the back of the room and present to the backs of the girls. There was no eye contact. One of the girls said to me,

"We can't even be FRIENDS with boys, teacher."

This was the first time they were in a class together, and it wasn't working. The girls would ignore the boys, and vice-versa.

There were separate stairways for male and female students and separate cafeterias. There were even separate sections in the library. The girls came to class by bus, and the boys would come in cars. The boys used to stay in hostels like the girls, but there was too much tribal violence that it was discontinued.

I did hear that there was a place they went to "make out", and there were even some pregnancies. The girls were never allowed to keep the babies because it would bring a huge amount of shame on their families.

The Tribes — Wasta

"Wasta" is a name for power and influence in the Middle East. Some tribes have it, and some don't. If they were born into another tribe without wasta, no matter how hard they worked students could not get ahead. One of the boys explained this to his teacher.

This (wasta), can cause problems for the teachers. One of my students, distantly related to the Sultan, described as a "Nasty piece of work" by another teacher, took a dislike to me. I was never told why, but she would sit and glare at me from her seat.

She went to the Dean of the university to complain, and said if I was not removed from the classroom she would "Take it higher". Because of her status, I suppose, and the fact that students had more power than teachers I was sent to staple teaching materials together. What a waste of skills!

But after a couple of weeks the teacher taking my place said he had had enough of that class, and I was asked to go back. It was described as a "shit class" by my teaching partner.

We teachers would often be treated like servants by the students. If there was a dispute, the teacher was usually found in the wrong. We had to have our paperwork up to date, so we could document any problems. So when I am asked about my favourite country I say Oman, but not for the teaching.

The Rebel

One of the girls was very modern and unconventional. She came from a powerful family, and definitely had a lot of wasta. She refused to wear an abaya and would sit by the pool in a bikini smoking. She said the students in the hostel didn't like her.

She was a very good student, though. She graduated with high marks and became a teacher at Nizwa University! She moved in with a teacher from Italy and lived common law.

Studying?

The students were there most days, but weren't serious about studying. So why did they come to university? To get out of the house and to socialize with their friends. Also, they would get a higher bride price with a university degree. Very few of them really cared about getting an education. I used to teach for the five or ten percent who were motivated.

One day the students really tried my patience for almost two hours; talking, interrupting, and not listening to the lesson. We were not allowed to shout, but they could tell by my demeanor that I was not happy.

"Why you angry, teacher?" one girl asked, so I tried the Arabic for "Listen to me"- "Ismaoonee." They all laughed because I pronounced it wrong!

The Arabic term for "forbidden" is "Haram." I tried to explain to the students that the teacher's desk was Haram, but they wouldn't accept it. They would even look through the teacher's briefcase at exam time if he or she left it in the classroom.

We had cubicles, and mine was my one private place away from the students. One day I turned the corner to find a group of girls in MY space, and one of them sitting in MY chair! I was very annoyed.

"WHAT are you doing here?"

"Teacher, we brought you a gift!"

This disarmed me completely, and I gratefully opened the makeup they had bought me. There was no special occasion, and they were just being nice.

An Invitation to Tea

Senan, my teaching partner and I were invited to the home of one of our students, Eptisam, for tea. I wore a nice dress, but didn't realize we were going sight-seeing and would be climbing up and down hills! We went in two cars, to accommodate everybody, and, as usual the men were in one car and the women in another one.

Sayed, Eptisam's father, could speak English, which he learned on board ship when he was in the Omani Navy. He picked us up and took us to his house and small date farm. There were several different varieties of dates on their farm, and his family sold them when they were ripe.

I didn't see Eptisam around, but when I looked up, there she was, barefoot, and up in a tree! She may have been picking the fruit to serve to us.

They were very welcoming and we had a delicious meal. After lunch Said's wife was gone for a long time. She came back with an Omani outfit for me! It was orange with jodphur like pants and a long decorated top. We were invited to this house a couple of times, and I met Said when I was living in Ibra and he was travelling through. He was one Omani who was always polite and respectful with me.

Hamoud

Another Omani who treated me with respect was Hamoud. Hamoud is a taxi driver, and I met him when I called a taxi to go to Muscat. We were going on vacation and I had two other teachers with me. The taxi didn't come to my apartment, so we had to hail him down for our ride.

He took a liking to me, and became my "Go to" taxi driver to go to Muscat, two hours away, or anywhere else. If he was busy he always apologized. I felt safe with him and used his services whenever I could until I bought my own vehicle.

We became friends, and after a few months or so, he invited me to come to his place for lunch. I met his large family, and felt honored to be invited. After lunch it was nap time. There was a big pile of mattresses in another room and they were spread on the floor. I lay down on one in the room with his wife and daughters and a little later Hamoud came to the door to take me home. I felt welcomed by this family. Omanis are known for their hospitality.

Sometime later he was in jail; I didn't know the details, but it had something to do with drinking- a serious offence in a Muslim country. I never did find out the details but he told me he liked drinking whiskey. Not a good pastime for a taxi driver!

My New Apartment

After six weeks in the Majan Guest House our apartment was ready. It was fully furnished, with marble floors, and beautiful oval shaped doorways, Arab style. It was also very dusty. I hired a cleaner, Das, who did a wonderful job, and didn't charge a lot. My place was big, with three bedrooms: it was big enough for a large family.

Several shacks outside the building housed the workers who had built our apartment, but when we moved in they had not completed the wall around the building. Every house or apartment had these walls for privacy. The first morning I looked out the window and saw a man outside shaving with a mirror tacked onto his wall. It was probably too dark in his tin shack.

A few days later I heard a noise outside and looked out. There was a bulldozer flattening the little village outside! In a few minutes there was no trace of it! The workers had either got another job or gone back to India.

Social Life in Nizwa

I spent three of my seven years in Oman in Nizwa. There was lots to do socially, as there were three colleges, with an average of 50 foreign teachers at each one. We used to congregate at the Falaj Daris Hotel, a five-minute drive from my apartment. "Falaj" was named after the complicated underground water system in Oman, and "Daris," for King Darius the Great of Persia, known for his great building projects.

The hotel had two swimming pools and a nice restaurant as well as al fresco dining around the pool.

Every month we had a Trivia Night-friendly competition among the colleges, and we took turns hosting the event. It was a lot of fun, with beer, wine and good food.

We also had a Writer's Group that met every two weeks. There were no restrictions on the writing, and we critiqued each other's work. Bjorn, from Sweden, wrote a story set in America, but the vocabulary was in British English, which was quickly pointed out-- lift, boot, etc.

David, from Wales, ran the group, and would always begin with "What's on top?" or

"What's on your mind this week?" It was a good ice-breaker.

Alternate weeks were taken up with the "Talking Stick," a native American custom in which only one person would speak at a time. This was the person holding the "stick"- a wooden spoon in our case. It was a multicultural group, and we always had a topic. One was on cities, and the speaker, Fatima, spoke about her hometown of Hyderabad. She described it so well that we were all ready to book flights there immediately! India was only three hours away so it was quite conceivable.

Trip to Yemen

There was a lot going on socially, but I had never been to the Middle East before, and was anxious to visit some of the countries nearby. One was Yemen, said to be "National Geographically beautiful." We had five days off during Ramadan, which fell just after we had started teaching, and I had a chance to go with two other female teachers. We packed up for a five-day trip.

We met the two Yemeni guys in an SUV at the border, and the adventure began. One was the driver and one was the guide. They were friendly and spoke pretty good English.

We were greatly overcharged in US dollars, so it was a good thing we were only there for five days.

Qat

The accommodation was clean and quiet, but one thing we noticed right away was that the guys were always chewing something, and it wasn't gum. It was ghat- pronounced "cat" and it's a very popular chewing leaf. A lot of the Arabic translations into English had several different spellings, thus, qat could be spelled ghat, or cat.

It is known as "Yemen's Narcotic Chewing Leaf" or "The Devil's Tea," by some and by others as a "feel good drug." It's part of every social event, from company meetings to weddings, which explains why so many people, adults and children both, have fat cheeks like squirrels. It reminded me of LSD in the '60s.

This drug is illegal in many countries but not in Yemen. It's a very poor country, and I think that ghat is the opiate of the masses, as vodka has been in Russia for a long time.

Positive comments include:

"Focuses the Mind; It relaxes you! it gives you energy! You can study better! It aids communication!" "It's just like salad," "It makes me feel euphoric! It's magic!"

But there are many negative aspects: insomnia, liver disease, psychosis, schizophrenia and even cancer, from toxins in the liver. Entire forests are devoted to the growth of qat, and the water supply is down because it's used for watering qat trees.

A protest group called "Khat Free Nation" says that khat "Is a threat to our future." They are conducting an awareness campaign in the schools.

Our driver offered some to me and I chewed it for a minute or two, but I didn't feel anything, just a slightly bitter taste. I think you have to keep on chewing to get a rush from it. (I just looked up qat in 2021, and todays' headline says that while other shops are closed due to COVID 19, the qat shops are still open. (Dec.6 2021) It seems it is still a serious problem in Yemen. Or not- depending whether you are a qat chewer!

A highlight for me was our trip along the Hadramout, that stretches all the way up to Oman. It is called the "Grand Canyon" of the Middle East. To my surprise, an armed guard joined us for our journey along the Hadramout, as we were heading into a dangerous area. He was carrying a Kalashnikov, and insisted on sitting in the front seat. This guard didn't socialize with us, or even smile, even when we asked if he could sing. I guess he took his job very seriously and I was glad when he left us.

While the guard was in our vehicle our tour guide had to squeeze himself between our bags in the back, but he didn't complain for the miles and miles it took us to descend from there.

After the guard left us my two friends fell asleep, and there I was, with a qat-chewing driver flying along the narrow track. I felt nervous because of the rapid speed he was going, and it was bumpy and uneven. I was relieved when we were back on level ground.

As we descended to the lower areas we saw women in pointed hats working in the fields. In their black dresses they looked like witches, and my friend Barbara got ready to take a photo; but she put her camera down after the woman grabbed a stone and raised it in the air. Like our students in Oman, Yemeni women don't like their photos taken.

A Camel in the Restaurant

Whenever we stopped for a meal, we were ushered into the ladies' section of the restaurant with no windows. I didn't like this, and felt claustrophobic. One had a camel's head in the window! Not just a picture, or a bust, but a real camel's head with blood around its neck. It was a beautiful young animal with its big brown eyes wide open. I felt sad looking at it, but I can't protest too much as I am not a vegetarian and camel meat has been on the menu in that part of the world for centuries.

Honey Shopping

Another incident that didn't endear me to Yemen was a shopping trip to a small town famous for its honey, according to our guide. We lined up with all the local people, and the shopkeeper was doing a roaring business, taking the money and handing over the jars of honey. No receipts. I bought three jars, for me and two of my neighbours back in Oman, and walked out of the little stall where the selling was going on. Suddenly there was a commotion.

"He says you haven't paid," said our guide.

I had just put my money away, and now, while writing this, I am thinking maybe I took out the money and put it away again. I was so convinced that I had paid at the time!

There was a lot of discussion in Arabic, and we decided to just leave, but the entire town followed us and and surrounded our vehicle. It was scary, and I just wanted to get out of there, so I took out my money and paid again and they let us pass. The guide said he believed the seller, so maybe I did make a mistake, or maybe it was a chance to get some money from the "rich foreign tourist" visiting their town. Again, there was no receipt or bill.

Most of the towns we visited were dirty and the people didn't seem friendly. Maybe it was the poverty. I was glad to get back to the white-washed houses in Oman.

An Unusual Driving Lesson

After I was back in Oman for a few weeks I decided to buy a car. Being in the Gulf, cars and gas were very cheap. My Peugeot, only a year old, was less than $1200 US. Most of us female teachers had a vehicle, to avoid groping by some of the taxi drivers. A lot of them did not know how to behave with Western women, and this happened if the woman sat in the front seat. One teacher told me that she was in tears when she got out of a taxi.

I took driving lessons, as I hadn't driven for a while. After a lot of lessons in my new-to-me Peugeot, I noticed my instructor rubbing the front of his robe- his dishdasha, and I asked him what he was doing. I couldn't believe it, but he was masturbating through the cloth! "I haven't had sex for a long time" was his excuse, and this was probably true, as families tended to sleep all together, or men in one room and women in another. I should have gone right to the police station and reported him. We drove right by it.

A "Taxi" Driver

I did love my little car, and it handled beautifully. The only problem was, one day it started to smell like gas, and I took it in to the shop. They told me the fuel pump wasn't working and it wasn't built for the hot climate. I left it to be fixed, and it was still under warranty, but they didn't have a loaner. I was waiting for a bus to the university when a car stopped and offered me a ride. He said he was a taxi driver even though his car had no special markings. I asked him how much it was and he said three rials. ($7.50 US) I didn't have change and he said he didn't either. Then he put his hand on my leg and said, "No money." I told him to find the nearest ATM and paid him for the trip.

As I mentioned before, Western women were considered easy, and even though Muslims are legally allowed to have four wives most of them have only one, because it was too expensive to maintain multiple households.

When I was teaching the family tree, I asked the students to draw the tree for their family. I was surprised when one girl showed me hers with her father at the head and the two wives and their children below. I asked what they call the other wife and the answer was "aunty."

For Non-Muslims Only"

Muscat, the capital, was only a couple of hours away, and every week or two I would drive to the big city for groceries. I had never been to the superstore Carrefour, and used to shop there. Everything was available except for pork, which was found in only one store in a separate room with the sign, "Non-Muslims Only."

It had a lower ceiling than the rest of the store, and it was like going into the "Adult Movie" section of a video store. I bought some bacon and ham and the girl on the checkout asked me to push it through myself. Perhaps she thought it was too disgusting to touch.

Students' Complaints

Whenever we saw a group of students in one of the administrator's offices we would think: "Is it me? Are they complaining about me?"

Actually, one class liked me and they all went to tell the administration. But the complaints far outweighed the compliments.

Before you think that only bad teachers get complaints, in our school there were over 50 teachers, and every one of them was complained about by the students. Interestingly, over 70% of these complaints were from Bedouin students. They are more interested in caring for their animals than studying.

Just after we started teaching a student went to Carlos, our DOS, and complained about her teacher. When questioned, it turned out that she didn't like the desks. They were flimsy and had no place to store books. There was nothing wrong with the teacher and she just wanted a desk in another room! Luckily Carlos questioned the student carefully.

One of my colleagues spent a lot of time and effort on one class, and made a point of relating it to their culture. He couldn't understand why a student complained because it was an excellent class!

He went to Marcia, who was in charge at that time, and her answer was:

"Exams are coming up, and the student wanted to make herself look better in case she got a low grade."

Students with "Wasta" usually passed. We were told to lower marks in the high 40s, if they were a poor student, and they would be sure to complain as the passing mark was 50. It just took a phone call from a parent, (usually the father), and they would pass.

If a student didn't do well it was always the teacher's fault. I saw two of my students in the market during the holidays, and I didn't remember their marks. I asked them what level they were going into. One of the students glared at me:

"Level 2 (her previous level), because YOU failed me, teacher!"

I tried to make my classes fun and interesting, and the first day of Summer School we played a game. It was a lot of fun and everyone was laughing. I was reflecting on this on my way back to the teacher's room when I ran into Dr. Al Abadi, our boss, on my way. I was surprised to hear him say there had been a complaint about me. I wasn't even told what it was.

"It isn't looking good," he said.

There was no investigation. The students could vote on whether to change the teacher or not, and they voted me out. Even if they didn't agree the students would go along with the others. It was hard to deal with the herd mentality, where the students had more power than their teachers. I asked what the school wanted from the teachers, and I was told, "Keep the students happy."

This happened to me twice in Nizwa, and it was extremely upsetting. I think it was a power game with the students, and during the Arab Spring, I heard that the Nizwa students got rid of the dean!

"Too strict!" They said, but I think it is what they needed. This dean was a former military man, and he ruled with an iron fist. People said the school ran better when he was in charge.

Racism against Indian Workers

There were a lot of Indian workers at our school, and some were mistreated by the Omanis.

Once I saw a student throwing some money at a worker in the cafeteria. I asked him why he did that, and he said, "Indian, teacher!"

I told him that the worker was a person too, and I shared this incident with my class. One girl said she had learned something from me.

Ramadan

Soon after we arrived in Oman it was the holy month of Ramadan. I didn't think it would affect us much but it did. We were told not to eat or drink anything in front of a Muslim person, which made this difficult because we were still teaching. One morning at break time I wanted to have a drink from my water bottle under my desk, and the students were milling around as usual.

I said, "Don't you want to take a break and go out of the classroom?"

They asked me why and I told them I wasn't allowed to eat or drink in front of them. "Oh, no problem, teacher!"

Alcohol in Oman

Even though Oman was officially alcohol-free, alcohol was readily available. We just had to buy a passport and pay what we thought we would use for one month. The liquor stores had signs that said, "Eastern Trading Company," and had no windows. These stores were open all year except during the month of Ramadan. However, some of the teachers wanted to celebrate their birthdays during Ramadan, and they managed to do it by staying in a hotel in Muscat, and were able to order their drinks from room service.

My cleaner, Nellie, would often ask if I had any "balance." We were allotted so much a month to spend on alcohol, depending on what we had paid when we applied for the passport. If I had money left over I would buy a bottle for Nellie and her friends, as they were Philippino, and low earners. As low earners they were not allowed to buy a passport.

Trip to Malaysia

The first year I was in Oman I decided to go on a trip to Malaysia for my summer break. It looked very beautiful on TV and I fell for the promotional advertising. Dalyia, our office manager is Malaysian, and she gave me the name of a tour operator.

I booked a three-week trip to KL (Kuala Lumpur), Penang and Langkawi, a resort island. Malaysia is a very humid place, and in Penang I managed to walk to a place with a swimming beach. I decided to go back by boat, which would be cooler.

An Unwise Decision

There were some long-tailed boats in a row on the beach, and I booked a trip on one of them with an Arab family of seven. It was a very short trip-maybe ten minutes. I didn't realize the waves were so big, and as we motored around a bend and dropped the family off I asked if I could get off there as well. The boatman insisted on taking me to the next cove where my hotel was, but when the seven people got off the boat was unbalanced. He took me into the shallow water so I could jump off, and I was just about to leap into the shallow water when a big wave capsized the boat and I was underneath it! It was very scary, but the next wave took the boat away from me and I was able to wade to shore.

There was the boat, on the beach, upside down, and the boatman was trying to flip it over by himself. He was quite a small guy and it was hard for him. I ran up the stairs for help, and a girl from Canada came back with me. She told me she had lifesaving experience and could help. She and the guy from the boat flipped the boat, and I started looking for my bag. Gas canisters and other nautical paraphernalia were strewn all over the beach, but there was no sign of my bag or my credit cards and money.

Kind Canadians

I had already paid for my room, but I had ordered room service and some other charges were pending. The girl and her husband, from Calgary, paid my bill and lent me some money so I could continue my journey to Langkawi. I was able to call my bank in Oman and have some money wired to me, and ended up staying with their family for a few days after I came back from Langkawi.

A Lucky Invitation/Lives Saved

They were missionaries, and were staying in Malaysia to teach at one of the schools. They also volunteered to help when the tsunami hit the island, and travelled to Acha to help with the rescue and recovery operation. They had a house close to the beach, and said that usually they would be relaxing on the beach on a Sunday with their kids. But on that day, the day the tsunami hit, they were invited to another part of the island to visit some friends, and this invitation probably saved their lives!

I enjoyed Malaysia and the Malaysians. One morning a man sweeping the street said good morning to me, and he wasn't trying to sell me anything!

My Father's Death

In 2007 my father died. I had been getting emails from a social worker in Hawaii where he had lived for the last few years. He said not to wait too long to visit him, as he might not live much longer.

We were just starting our school year, and were not teaching any classes yet, so I asked for compassionate leave to visit my dad. I was still in China visiting David. The school in Nizwa said I could go, but they would not pay me because I had not filled out the required form. I flew to Honolulu from China, with the help of my friend Carman, who found me a seat on Cathay Pacific.

I hadn't seen my dad in over five years. He was in a wheelchair, and needed to be fed and dressed, but otherwise he was in good spirits and still had his sense of humour. His mind was clear as a bell.

It was one month before his 94th birthday, and his caregiver, Elizabeth, decided to have a party for him, as we didn't know if he was going to be around the following month. He begged off, saying he couldn't do it, and my cousin, who had come from England to help, said this was very rude, but she didn't know he was going to pass away a couple of days later.

A home care nurse came to assess him at that time and she said he would probably pass away that same day. He had liver disease, from his wild living as a young man. He had stopped drinking when he was about 30, but apparently the damage was done.

A former pilot, he went to the US when he and my mother broke up. I was four. He never remarried. He told me he proposed to a flight attendant friend of his, and her response was:

"Bill, I'm not the marrying kind, and you're not the marrying kind either. Let's not spoil a good friendship."

He passed away that evening, and his body, with the open mouth, was not my father. I didn't think his body had anything to do with him, but when the men came to take him away I didn't let them cover his face. Maybe it was him after all.

We had a small sendoff at the old folks' home and I was given a pin that was a memento of his membership in "The Quiet Birdmen" an association of former pilots who had flown over a million miles.

Dad and "Old Blue"

After I returned to Oman the lawyer in the US informed me that he received $3000 for a painting of my Dad's. It was by a famous Dutch painter named Leetag who painted on black velvet, and Dad had bought the painting of a fisherman as an investment. I decided to go to Europe with this money. It was a good trip, in the summer, and I found the countries charming.

Back in Oman

I decided to start my trip in Belarus to visit my friend Vera and her family. Back in Oman at the writer's group, when David asked "What's on top? I said, "My visa to Belarus." I was having trouble getting one, but I was able to get one on arrival in the end.

When I told another teacher I was going to Belarus, he said he knew some dancers from Belarus right there in Nizwa! I picked up some gifts for their families who came to pick them up at my hotel in Minsk. They had no English, but brought me a chocolate bar for my trouble.

My Trip to Europe

I had planned to visit seven countries and started out in Belarus. My friend Vera was there, who I had met in China where she was teaching English. She had a little boy, Yegor, and wanted me to stay at their house in Minsk. I like my privacy and decided to stay in a hotel, and I was glad I did because their place was very small. People there combine their living rooms and bedrooms, with pull out couches.

Belarus

When I arrived in Belarus, one thing I noticed was there was no English anywhere! As Belarus used to be part of Russia there were lots of Russian signs, but no English translation. My hotel room was clean and comfortable, but I didn't meet any other foreigners.

Belarussian Men

My hotel was in a beautiful park, surrounded by trees. The first morning I went for a walk in the park and sat on a bench. A guy sat down very close to me, too close. There was no conversation, but I finally left the bench to him.

A few days later we were invited to Vera's sister's for dinner. I wanted to pick up a bottle of wine, so we went to the liquor store. A man blocked my way on one of the aisles. I couldn't move in any direction. He kept saying something in Russian but I didn't understand him. He was good looking, but I was glad to finally get away.

Still another incident happened when I got off a bus and I couldn't find my hotel. There was a couple sitting on a wall, and I showed them my key, and asked in sign language if they knew where it was. They directed me and I thought that was the end of it, but the next day someone told me the man had called the hotel and asked about me, and wanted to meet me! He showed up at the hotel looking for me. I escaped. I was flattered by the attention!

Vera's mom had a dacha, a country house, and we were invited there for a couple of days. It was fun going there, and I loved her mom's cooking! A lot of dachas have spas that the people run to across the snow in the winter.

Lithuania

My next destination was Lithuania, where I only stayed for a few days so my visa would be valid. There was a big music festival going on, and I wanted to attend. It didn't happen even though I took a long bus trip to get there. It was so overcrowded that I was unable to get accommodation, and finally someone helped me find a place for the night, back in Vilnius, the city I had left from! Two long bus trips in one day! I did go on a tour of Vilnuis, the charming capital, and enjoyed the greenery.

Poland

I left for Poland next, visited lovely Kracow, and then Warsaw. Auschwitz was a chilling experience, with piles of grey hair shaved off the prisoners. I saw Shindler's Factory, which was closed- and the Salt Mines, where we took a tiny, crowded elevator underground. I could touch the stones and lick the salt from my fingers.
The elevator ride was frightening, with a lot of people cramped together like the cattle cars that took so many people to their deaths!

Back in Kracow it was mid-summer; the weather was beautiful and the trees and flowers were in full bloom. Lots of tourists and lots of signs offering "Alkohol!" Europe was charming, with its ornate architecture, tasty food and friendly people. Flower baskets were hanging everywhere. The horror of the Jewish genocide was a grisly contrast- all those lives lost and families torn apart!

Hungary

My next stop was Hungary, to visit my friend from Nizwa, Georgina. She had an MA in English from Montreal, so even though she was Hungarian she was well qualified to teach English. She was working to pay for her daughter's education. She and her family come from Budapest, a charming city, divided into two sections, Buda and Pest. They lived in the nicer part – Buda. I had some tasty goulash at Georgina's house, where her son William made me tea with milk, with a great flourish. They drink out of glass cups without milk, but William gave me a china cup for mine-perhaps I was the first to use it!

I was very surprised to see the breakfast at my hotel. There it was-- all the meats, roast chickens, steaks, vegetables, a full course dinner at 7 am! Fine linens and tableware completed the tableau. There was even a bar in one section of the restaurant, with a customer already enjoying a drink!

A Lucky Break

I thought the money would be easy in Europe, as a lot of countries were using Euros, but all the countries I visited were in Eastern Europe where they were still using their own currencies. I thought I would be smart and use 2 wallets, one for the country I was travelling in, and the other one for my Canadian money and passport. One day I went out to do some food shopping, and checked the wallets when I got back to my room. I couldn't find the one with my passport! I looked through every pocket and bag I had, but came up with nothing.

"I must have left the wallet in the store." I thought.

Back at the store, I explained (with sign language), that I thought I had left my wallet there. No response. The woman just stared at me with a deadpan face.

I looked around the store and I was going to leave, but suddenly there was a crowd of people there.

"Can anyone here speak English?"

A quiet voice responded. "I can help you."

I told her my problem, and, once again we faced the shopkeeper, who said something in Hungarian then disappeared. Her face didn't show any emotion, and so I asked the woman translating what was going on.

"She has your wallet at the back of the store, and she will give it to you after she calls the owner."

What a relief! I really felt God was looking after me that time.

Another adventure in Hungary was my trip through the mountains on a train staffed by children! They did all the jobs on the train, except for driving, of course, and they had to keep their grades up at school to be able to do this. It was considered a great honor. I met a woman, her boyfriend and her elderly father, who they were taking out for the day. She was a teacher and spoke perfect English. We chatted all that day. Edit and I are still in touch on Facebook.

Time in Turkey

My next destination was Turkey, and I had planned to meet Shirley Smith, who had contacted me about teaching in Oman. We had never met in person, but that's the beauty of the internet- sometimes strangers become friends.

I liked Shirley right away, and found her to be an outgoing, gregarious lady. She wrote a book about her teaching and we all celebrated back in Oman the day the book was published! We all toasted her and her accomplishment!

She invited a couple we met on the subway to have dinner with us. They were looking for a restaurant, and asked if we knew of any good ones. "You might as well come along with us," said Shirley, and we all went to a wonderful rooftop restaurant for dinner. We had barbecued chicken, salads, and flat bread, and it was a delicious meal. I didn't know I would be sick a few hours later. I think a lot of the dishes were sitting out in the heat, as the restaurant was busy.

I had a chance to visit the famous Princess Islands the next morning. I knew I would not have another chance so, even though I wasn't feeling well I went to the ferry to meet up with some other people.

We had to sit on the ferry and wait for a long time, and there was food cooking. I was already feeling nauseous, and the smell of the food made it worse. I had to use a basket lined with a plastic bag. There were a lot of people on the boat, and a nice lady gave me a tissue and a bottle of water.

Back to Oman

After a month in Europe it was time to return to Oman and my teaching.

I had been thinking about Salalah, a city in the south of the country, with lovely beaches and lots of other schools. I applied to Dhofar University there and was hired sight unseen.

But just after I had paid my own way there one weekend and met some of the teachers, I got an email saying that my contract was cancelled, "Because you are 62 years old." I reminded them they could hire anyone they wanted, as they were a private university, but they wouldn't change their minds. I still had a few months left on my contract in Nizwa, so I started looking for other opportunities.

Cyclone Gonu 2007

Rain is an infrequent visitor to Oman. Some towns only get rain every four years! The first week of classes there was a rainstorm and the students wanted to go out and play. These were university students? One of the teachers did dismiss his class, and so we were pressured to let them all go.

One day the wadi was flooded, and the parking lot became a river. Families were sitting on the banks having picnics, and boys were riding their bikes through the shallow water. It was a Friday, a holiday anyway, and the rain cooled off the stifling temperature. It was a fun event for them, but for me, coming from Vancouver, one of the rainiest cities in the world, it was just another day of rain. I guess they feel that way about sunny weather. Just another sunny day! Ho hum!

But there was nothing like the cyclone of 2007: A Super Cyclone-- the first of its kind in Oman. It was classed as the worst natural disaster in Oman's history!

This happened on June 6, which was the end of our school year, and the end-of-year activities: a dinner and a play were cancelled. But by the time the storm reached Nizwa, two hours' drive from Muscat and the coast, it had subsided into a light drizzle.

Seven thousand workers were evacuated from the coastal island of Masirah, and this affected us swimmers, as these men, who were put up at our hotel, had never seen women in bathing suits before and stared at us. All the sun beds were taken inside, and so we had to put our belongings on the ground.

Muscat was badly hit, especially the low-lying areas and shorelines. The coastal road was washed out and a lot of the buildings on it including one of our favorite coffee spots.

A friend of mine who lived in Muscat said he saw a huge truck flying through the air! The Oman news reported there were only 50 deaths, but I heard from a reliable source that there were as many as 10,000. Muscat reported winds of 100 kilometres an hour, and there was $4 billion dollars' worth of damage and $200 million in loss of oil exports.

The Highway to Hell

Jocelyn and I were going to Muscat to visit our friend Polly who was in the hospital and have lunch along the way. It was a two-lane highway, and we didn't know that one lane was washed out. The two- lane highway was then only one lane, with the other lane blown away. I think most of the inhabitants of Nizwa were using the other lane. It was very crowded using only one lane! We passed a gas station with all the blacktop missing and a truck overturned.

Helicopters were buzzing over our heads and soldiers, who were monitoring the traffic had set up tents on the side of the road. We were stuck in traffic for two hours, barely moving, and were nowhere near Muscat. It's usually a two-hour drive. After the stress of stop and go traffic driving Jocelyn had finally had enough and we went back to Nizwa for lunch.

A lot of people on the road were taking water to Muscat for their family members there. The big water trucks were taking advantage of the emergency to cash in on some extra profits, but people who were overcharged were advised to get the number of those trucks and report them.

My church in Muscat was full of water, and my friend Arlene drove in from Nizwa to help sweep out the sanctuary, which was filled with debris and water four feet deep. All the damage was eventually repaired, and these days you would never know there had been such a catastrophe.

Chapter 6

Four Years in Salalah: The Sun, Sea and Safra

Because of the students' complaints, my Nizwa contract wasn't renewed. My DOS, Dr. Labadi, however, gave me a very good reference, and said the students should have waited until the contracts were renewed to complain. I think the complaining was a game with them, but it was hard to work under those conditions.

Whenever we saw a group of students in one of the administration offices, we never knew if they were complaining about us. The complaints about the teachers were taken seriously, even though many of them were lies.

A New Start

I was given a tip to contact a recruiter called Globnet, and they said they would try to find me a job in Salalah. It was late summer, the time everyone was applying for teaching jobs, and I was told that "It wasn't looking good" at SCOT, the Salalah College of Technology. We had a break and my friend Georgina and I flew to Jordan for a whirlwind tour of the country. We landed in Damascus, the oldest continuously inhabited city in the world. The airport needed refurbishing. We only had 4 days, and the highlight for me was floating in the Dead Sea and buying all the skin care products made from its mud.

On our way home, I remarked to Georgina that if the job in Salalah came through it would only be through divine intervention. I got the call the next morning.

"Are you ready to go to Salalah?" the voice on the phone said. I gave my notice at the Tourism College, and got ready to leave for Salalah. I was offered a free flight there and so I hired one of the taxi drivers to drive my car down there.

The first time I had gone to Salalah I went with 2 male teachers, one with the famous name of Neil Armstrong, and we took the bus. Men and women are not allowed to sit together unless they are related, so I sat next to a Nepali girl, who had very little English, and I had NO Napali. We smiled a lot. We had a good time at a hotel on the beach, and I was sorry to return to Nizwa.

Another couple, Martin and Nadjeili who taught at the Nizwa College of Technology moved to Salalah as well. The beach was a big factor in their decision.

The Plantation

The first few days I was put up at a hotel. Someone had left a lot of things in the drawers, and I threw a lot of them out, and then I was told it was a room belonging to one of the hotel staff. They were full so he vacated his room for me. I stopped throwing his belongings away, and felt I should have reimbursed him for his loss.

I retrieved my car, loaded with my stuff, and started driving around looking for more permanent accommodation. I pulled into a place with a lot of greenery around the entrance, and talked to a woman who lived there. She gave me the number of the owner, and I moved in to "The Plantation."

Papayas, bananas, kiwi fruit and lots of coconut palms were everywhere, and even though the apartments were fairly old, the floral surroundings made it delightful. It was near the beach and The Crowne Plaza Hotel, and swimming pools! I could have a dip before my teaching day started! One morning, about 6 am I was walking my dog and heard a noise from a palm tree up above. There were two men there-throwing coconuts to the ground and the other one bundling them up in fishnet! This gave me quite a start! I thought they were stealing but Wasu told me they had paid for the fruit.

Wasu, the caretaker, was an Indian man, who had worked there for years, and he was a bit bow-legged. He took care of collecting the rents, gardening and anything else around the property. When I arrived he was living in a small house with his brother. I found out later that there was no toilet in his place. I was shocked at this, but he didn't seem to mind.

Soon after he told me they were going to India because another brother was getting married. The day they were leaving his brother was all ready to go and he wasn't. He said he was going later, but, in fact, the owner had said he couldn't go. I was very angry, but I didn't say anything to the owner Sheikh Salim, who was always very sweet and charming to me. He would cut a fresh coconut whenever I had guests so we could drink the fresh juice. There was no comparison between fresh and bottled juice!

He was very money oriented, and during the Khareef – and the cooler season he made a lot of money by doubling the rents for the visiting Saudis, who came to visit in droves during the 3 months of cooler weather. He had already told me I didn't have to pay for the weeks I would be away in the summer, but one of the tenants left without paying his rent (he had asked repeatedly for a new air conditioner as he and his family were sweltering in the heat but never received one.)

Just before I was to leave for my vacation, he said that he would offer me my apartment for only 400 Rials, during the cooler Khareef season. He said he could get 1200 for my apartment at that time, as most of the apartments were rented to wealthy Saudis and their families. That was twice as much as I was paying- 200 Rials. He must have thought I was really stupid!

I only had one week left until my vacation, so Safra and I moved into one of the dusty one-room cottages at the back of the property. I was glad to hear that he wasn't able to rent my place while I was away.

Safra

A stray dog gave birth to some puppies on the Sultan's farm nearby and the Indian workers used to feed them. They thought that the Omanis were going to harm them, as dogs are considered evil and dirty in their culture, and started asking around if anyone would like to adopt one. I took the female, and called her Safra, the Arabic word for yellow, as she was a yellowy-brown colour.

The first couple of days she just lay on the couch, and thought, "This is going to be easy," and started putting newspapers on the kitchen floor.

When the vet came to examine her she said she would come back in September when she was six months old to spay her, as she was only four months old at the time.

Nelly, my cleaning lady, said her friend could look after Safra for me, and would send me photos on Facebook. Some other friends offered to store my furniture, and I thought I was all set for my holiday, but I didn't expect a big surprise when I came back to pick up my dog.

When I came back from my holiday in Canada a few weeks later I noticed her stomach was dragging down and her nipples were swollen. I called the vet, and she said to bring her in right away.

This was easier than it sounded. We were at least a seven- hour drive from Muscat, and she didn't have the paperwork to fly, so my friend Alan and I drove all night to get to the vet on Wednesday, as this was the only day they did spaying for dogs. Alan got Tuffy from his next-door neighbour, an Omani man. When his wife saw the dog she said it was "unislamic" to have a dog and to give him away.

We drove all night on the bumpy road and arrived in Muscat just as the sun was coming up. The air conditioner stopped working at the same time. Both dogs were panting in the back of my small car, and to top this off we got lost. After a stressful half hour we found the clinic and dropped both dogs off there.

Alan and Tuffy on the beach

Tuffy had been well behaved all the way, but I guess the trip was just too much for him, and we got a call from the vet to say that he was guarding the reception desk and wouldn't let the receptionist sit down!

During the surgery they found eight fetuses in Safra's belly, and they all died. As Elke, the vet said, "What would you do with eight puppies?" (This was in a country that doesn't like dogs.)

When we picked Safra up the next day she came out of a lower cage with her tail going like a windmill, wearing a ruffle around her neck like Queen Elizabeth 1. We were so glad to see each other!

The man who had been taking care of her said he didn't know how this happened, but Nelly told me that she got out for 3 days. Three days of partying!

While Alan had a much-needed rest, as he had done most of the driving, I drove the stifling car across town to the Peugeot dealer. A nice man came into the showroom and asked if he could help me. I blurted out that we had driven all night and the air con had stopped working and we had two panting dogs in the back.

He was the manager, and said he would see what he could do. When it came time to pay the bill there wasn't one, as it was a quick job and it was just a matter of filling up the gas. I think it was because it was an easy job and also because he was a nice guy. His name is Simon Harle.

Alan didn't get Tuffy neutered but did a few months later. He was off on Wednesdays, so he would call and ask if I wanted to take Safra over to play with Tuffy. So he looked after the two dogs, fed them and even clipped Safra's nails. Nice guy!

Passport Problems: Illegal Action

We all had recruiters who helped us get our teaching positions. They were paid handsomely for it too, about $1900 USD per teacher, including our salaries. Mine, Globnet, had a policy of keeping the teachers' passports until the end of the year.

A lot of the teachers were from India and the Philippines and were used to this treatment but I wasn't. I was using a UK passport at the time as I was born in England, and I called the UK Embassy about it. I was told that the passports belonged to the UK government and for the recruiter to keep the passports was illegal.

The second year I called the director of the recruiting firm, and he seemed quite friendly until I told him I didn't want to surrender my passport. He told me I didn't have to, but not to tell any of the other teachers.

When my contract wasn't renewed I think it was because they thought I was a trouble-maker.

The Beach: Saving a Life

I was out of a job again, but was hired by a language school, even though the ad said "Nobody over 55." Sometimes looking younger is an asset.

I was working afternoons and evenings again, and was able to swim in the mornings after my trips to the beach with Safra. I took her to the beach every morning, but when April, the hottest month arrived we would go at five, because it was too hot and humid by seven.

Early one morning I saw something moving near a rock, and as I got closer I realized it was a baby turtle! He was waving his fin at the rock and hitting it. I picked up the little guy, brushed the sand off and then carried him over and put him into the water. I felt proud of myself for saving a life!

Another morning I saw a man fishing, with his wife watching from a lawn chair. He threw a fish to Safra, and she gobbled it up. He then threw a couple more for her to feast on.

Beachside Yoga

We teachers would socialize at The Crowne Plaza Hotel, which was close to my place and the beach. Some of us would join Steve, a teacher from Dhofar University for free yoga classes on the lawn. It was good exercise, but I had trouble balancing in the tree position. I also met Toni at the Crowne. She was a hair stylist from China and we became friends. We met again in China years later.

Chapter 7

Ibra: A Year and a Half

My contract was not renewed, but I was hired at A'Sharqiya University which was only two years old. The university was in Ibra, a land-locked town only a couple of hours from Muscat. A moving van took me, my furniture and Safra all the way from Salalah. It was a twenty-hour trip, with Safra sleeping on a little shelf behind the driver.

We moved into an apartment across from Bill, a friend from Salalah, who would bring his lamb bones from the Turkish Restaurant for my dog(s). (Explanation later).

The second year I rented a house on a wadi with four bedrooms and a lovely landlord, who visited me weekly with eggs and dates from his garden. I couldn't eat all the dates myself, so I would make the rounds and offer them to the other teachers.

Most of us were new to Ibra, and the first year we had a wonderful boss called Jim, an American, who was very supportive of us teachers. There wasn't much to do in Ibra, but it was only two hours away from Muscat where all the fun was.

We sometimes went to the Sharqiya Sands Hotel, about a twenty-minute drive from Ibra, but the pool was full of sand. Maybe that's why it was called "The Sands?"

We enjoyed swimming at the hotel pools in Muscat and dining at the buffets afterwards. One weekend I went to Muscat with a couple of the guys. We ordered Margaritas, and I was stirring mine to find the alcohol. Don finally asked the waiter if there was any alcohol in our drinks.

"Oh, no, sir!"

One of the guys ordered a cheeseburger. When he got his order, there was only a piece of cheese in a hamburger bun. When he asked about the meat, the answer was, "If you want meat you have to ask for a meat burger!"

Losing Safra

I had had Safra for three years when we moved to Ibra, and I was very attached to her. I had only been there for a week, and I wanted to visit the famous Wadi Tiwi. Its emerald pools and mountain scenery are famous for locals and tourists alike, and I couldn't wait. It was just over an hour's drive away, and I since I had sold my car in Salalah I hired a taxi to go there. I invited a teacher from South Africa, Martin, and he asked if Roman from Quebec could come along. I didn't realize this invitation would cause me to lose my dog!

Safra was used to my little blue Peugeot, but she happily got into the front of the taxi with me. I put her on the floor, as she was a full-grown dog by this time, and she climbed up on my lap. She licked my face when she saw the mountains.

When we arrived at our destination, we had to walk on logs to get to the swimming area. I was carrying dog food and clothing, and had Safra on the leash. The guys had gone ahead and were out of sight. Why didn't I yell?

It was too difficult to try to manage my things and Safra so I let her off the leash. This was a big mistake. We had to cross a bridge to get there and she was afraid to cross, and kept looking for a place to swim to where we were. Looking terrified, she finally swam across the pond, with her eyes wide open and her ears back.

We spent the afternoon there, and I swam in the water, but Safra wouldn't go back in. She wouldn't come to me when we started packing up to leave, and we walked across the bridge calling to her.

We were all waiting in the taxi when she finally crossed the bridge, and she trotted over to the car. She was just about to jump in with me when she turned her head, saw the two guys in the back and bolted. I thought that she would be waiting for me if I went back in the morning but there was no sign of her when I went back the next morning.

I went back there at least ten times, offered rewards gradually increasing in value, and prayed a lot. Every time we went there the locals said she was fine, and not to worry that they would feed her. They told me she howled at the moon every night.

Gypsy and Wahiba

I had gotten used to having a dog around the house, and it was just too lonely without the patter of little feet in my apartment. A few weeks later I went to the animal shelter to pick up another dog. Two wadi dogs, a male and a female had just been put in a cage together because they got along so well together. Gypsy was the female and an older dog, and Wahiba was the male, who had the same markings and looked almost exactly like Safra. I brought

My Three Dogs and Me

them both back to my home in Ibra. One of the teachers, Charles, drove us there and back, but when he stopped "So the dogs could relieve themselves", they stayed put.

Mango

It was so good to have someone to come home to again, and I was surprised when I got a call one day to say,

"I have your dog."

I didn't think it was likely that it was Safra, as she wouldn't let anyone near her, but I agreed to meet the guy at a coffee shop an hour later. A young white dog was lying in the back seat, NOT Safra, but I agreed to take her home because I didn't know what the guy would do to her.

She was very docile, and came with me on the leash I had brought. The other dogs sniffed and licked her all over, and everything was fine for a while, with all three dogs sleeping on my bed. Good thing it was a king size!

I called the new dog Mango, and she soon became my favorite. She was a very affectionate puppy, and grew up to be a very affectionate dog. Unfortunately, as she got older, she started challenging Gypsy at the food bowl, resulting in some horrendous bloody fights! I resorted to throwing water on them, and once I hit them on the head with a broom before they would stop. I had to separate the two dogs and once I even had to take Gypsy to the vet in Muscat. She was unable to walk after one of these fights, and Mango's white chest was like a butcher's apron, all covered with blood. We all went for walks in the wadi together, but kept them a few feet apart. I thought they were going to kill each other!

I spent hours on the phone with Alfa, the dog trainer in Muscat, who gave me a lot of good advice. Finally, after a few days of fighting, the situation was resolved.

I would put the three food bowls down; and Mango and Wahiba would wait on the floor until Gypsy had eaten hers. They would lie down on the floor until she had sampled their food before they ate. She was the queen again!

The Arab Spring 2011

When the Arab Spring started in Tunisia we didn't think it would come to Oman because it's a peaceful country. We were wrong. One morning we noticed banners in Arabic script hanging from trees all over the campus, and I was just starting my class when a male student burst in and addressed the class in Arabic.

Then he looked at me, and said,

"There is no class."

I still didn't get it until someone came and said that there was a meeting with one of the deans. He told us there were going to be demonstrations, and told us to go home "For your own safety."

We were invited back the next day, and had a meeting with the dean of the university. He started to say this was the teachers' fault, but Don, a former lawyer, who was just waiting to interrupt, shouted at him, and told him in no uncertain terms that this was untrue.

"Thank you for your speech." Dr. Fauzi countered.

We had three former lawyers on staff, one South African, one Canadian, and one American, Don, who was the only one who got involved in our meetings.

Termination of Contract

At the end of the year we had a meeting with our recruiter, ELS, and they told us that we were all terminated, as the university hadn't renewed THEIR contract.

They told us not to apply directly to the university, as "There would be consequences", but I applied anyway. I had completed my Master's degree, and they seemed pleased with that, even though it was an online qualification. They hired me to teach the following year.

After my holiday in China, I returned to Oman for my last year. I had planned to return to Canada, and wanted to save money for a modest house somewhere.

It wasn't to be. My nice DOS wasn't rehired, and we had an Arab DOS who had been fired the first year. He changed our classes four times, and we were all feeling stressed out. One day I yelled at my students for not doing their homework, and they all went to complain.

I had a party on the Sunday that week, and most of the teachers attended. I had no idea that my contract would be broken the next day, or that one of my colleagues would die.

Jeff

The next morning as I was on my way to school, I passed two of the female teachers. They had said not to pick them up, because they had been getting a ride with Jeff, and Caroline smiled sadly as I passed them. I found out later he hadn't showed up that morning and so they called his landlord, who opened his door, and they found Jeff's body on the floor inside. They think it was a heart attack. How sad! When I looked at his photo, taken at my party, I was shocked by the paleness of his skin. We had a small service. His name was Jeffery Teacher, and he was a good teacher and a good friend.

That same day there was a termination letter waiting for me. It was dated December 25, but I didn't point this out, even though it was then October. I was told that the man who received the complaints took all the notes to the dean of the university. Gone were my dreams of buying a house!

I stayed in Ibra for several more weeks to find homes for the three dogs. I loved them like my own children. I didn't have a home to take them to, and didn't even know where I was going after leaving Oman. One of the Phillipino guys from the college asked if he could adopt Mango, and he came to take her back to his home. When I saw him leaving with her on the leash I felt a painful tug on my heart. One day I asked him if I could keep her overnight. Mango started whimpering in the morning, so we went to visit the other dogs and went for a walk with them. A nurse from church, Babitha, had said she would ask around at the hospital, and the following week said that one of the girls had offered to take the other two dogs. It seemed to be working out well, and I felt better about leaving them with someone to care for them. But the very next morning, the girl called me and said her room-mates objected to having them, and that she couldn't keep them. What was I going to do?

I called John, who had Mango, and he agreed to take the other two. I didn't realize that when he left them alone outside his house all day that barking would be a problem, and that he would also leave them alone at night while he socialized with his friends. Within a month he had taken the two older dogs back to the shelter, and "avoided the question" when he was asked about Mango. I hope she survived.

Chapter 8

Goodbye Oman, Hello India!

After staying in Oman for several weeks, working on my fitness and finding a home for the dogs I was finally ready to leave.

Mohammed, the maintenance man, came to drive me to the airport. I asked him to stop at the store to buy treats, and at John's house, so I could give them to the dogs and say goodbye. They were behind a fence, but I was able to slip the treats through the bars, pet their noses and get my fingers licked.

There was a night flight to Dubai and another flight early the next morning. The hotel was $200 US, but I spent the money and it was well worth it. The other alternative was the lounge, with slippery plastic lounge chairs in a noisy room. I was thankful to have my own soft bed and shower.

David had invited me back to China, and I was happy to see him but it was winter and cold and rainy. I missed my sunny bungalow in Oman.

I tried to find work in China, but it wasn't to be, even though Pastor Gabe posted my credentials on the church website. I went back to eslcafe.com, where I had found several jobs in the past. This website, developed by Dave Sperling, was a great resource for job seekers in the education field.

One post that appealed to me was near the Himalayas in India. I had visited that country in the south, and northern India appealed to me. So did the organization-- Tibet Charity. It was a volunteer job for five months, and our students were Tibetan monks living in exile in Dharamsala. The temple and residence of their spiritual leader, the Dalai Lama, was just a few steps away from our school.

The charity didn't offer to pay the airfare or accommodation, and the only benefit was a free vegetarian lunch every day. But the post stimulated my adventurous spirit, and it turned out to be a wonderful experience.

I had to fill out the paperwork in China. China and what used to be Tibet, are not on good terms, so I had to be very careful filling out the application. I did not say what I was going to do in India, and I certainly didn't mention going to work for an organization connected to the Dalai Lama, who they say is an evil man. How could they?

Incredible India

A Happy Time in India

With the help of a kind Chinese man at the embassy I filled out the long complicated form, and I was soon on a flight to Delhi, where I was to stay overnight and then take a bus for another 12 hours to Dharamsala. The guest house in Delhi was very basic and on a dirt road, but the room was clean and the staff were polite and friendly.

When I asked about the bus, I was told, "Take the Volvo bus. They're the best."

So I bought a ticket and boarded the bus with a lot of other people. I met a young woman who worked with stray dogs and said they were "So grateful" for the food and shelter provided for them.

I gradually nodded off to sleep, hoping to be in Dharamsala in the morning, but this was not to be. I was dreaming that someone was calling me, then when the bus driver started shaking my shoulder I was awake, and he was saying,

"Come, come!"

Come where? It was dark and cold outside, and I didn't want to get off. Someone said our bus had broken down, so I finally got off the bus, where we were to board another one. We handed our bags in through its window. Then someone decided it was too expensive, so all the bags were passed back out to us in the cold.

We waited for the city bus, which was a very old, rusty vehicle. One of the bus men gave me his seat, which was very kind. I enjoyed the mountain scenery once the sun came up, and it was beautiful to see its warming rays shining over the mountains.

After many turns around the mountainsides we saw a bus at the bottom of a cliff. It looked like it had been there a while, and I assumed it was left there as a warning to others not to speed on the hairpin turns.

We finally arrived in Mcleodjunj, our destination. The bus stopped in the square, and I had a lovely hot coffee before taking a taxi to Tibet Charity. It was just down the road, but I had all my bags with me.

The Charity was housed in a big stone house with lots of stairs. I found my way to the office, on the third floor, but didn't get a very warm greeting because I was supposed to be teaching a class, and someone had to fill in for me. No cell phones in those days.

Keldun in Champa Valley

Housing

I was taken to some cheap hotels in town. They were very basic, with no closets for my clothes. I didn't like any of them, but what the housing lacked in amenties it made up for in the million- dollar mountain scenery.

Keldun, a Tibetan-American guy, took me to the Green Hotel the first night where all the tourists hung out. I had my first taste of Tibetan food there- a hot tasty soup.

Its patio overlooked the beautiful valley below. A pretty blonde girl was sitting on this balcony working on a laptop and smiling. She was another colleague, Verena from Hamburg. Brij, an Indo-Canadian guy from Vancouver, slso joined us, and Eva from Austria came a few months later. We all became good friends. They didn't seem to mind that I was decades older.

Climbing Hills- The Open Sky

I went to the Open Sky Restaurant the next day at a hairpin turn in the road, that catered to tourists and locals, with of course another million-dollar view of the valley below. I ended up going every day and having a delicious parantha (an Indian style pancake with a potato filling) and coffee for breakfast.

Clifford

I met Clifford at that restaurant, a lovely Scottish gentleman, who would ride his bike up the steep mountain roads every day just to drink his tea while watching the sunrise over the valley. He lived further down the hillside, and would ride his bicycle uphill and around the turns overlooking the panorama below. He brought fireworks to my birthday party and set them off from the flat stone roof. It was the first time I enjoyed fireworks for the occasion. He became a part of our little group, and was a guest at Brij's wedding a few months later.

The restaurant overlooks the beautiful Champa Valley, and there was a notice tacked on the wall advertising a room nearby. I walked along a path that led to some houses, and found Kamila, the landlady. She showed me another very basic room for $100 a month. I took it, and hung my clothes on hooks on the wall- no closets or dressers, but Kamila gave me three small tables with drawers.

The first night there was a commotion in the bathroom, which had windows open to the sky, and there was a bird flying around! I managed to shoo the bird away, and I bought some small cushions the next day and stuffed the hole with one of them.

Kamala and Her Kids

A hot plate for cooking sat on a shelf but I didn't use it often. One night Kamila showed me how to make dhal. She's a widow, living with her five children: lovely kids, and they used to visit me often. They were all vegetarian. The youngest daughter lived with Kamila's parents, and when I asked why she lived with them, I was told that they didn't have any more children living at home and they "needed a child." In their free time the girls tutor the local kids from the village.

One morning I invited the youngest girl to have breakfast with me at the Open Sky. She was six at the time. When I asked her what she wanted she said, "Ice Cream!" We called her mom, who said no, but she still wanted ice cream. I refused, and she had no breakfast that day!

My First Class: Monks in Maroon, Lazy Students

When I had my first class the next morning I was greeted by a roomful of monks in maroon coloured robes. They were friendly guys, and good students, and we got along well. But as I was teaching the class I noticed that three of the students were sleeping in corners and not paying attention at all.

These were the canine members of the class, and were well-behaved, aside from the sleeping! Tibet Charity has a vet service, and the resident dogs used to live in the school until the neighbors complained about the barking. I'm not sure why these three were still living there, but they were no trouble, and when we went for walks they were good companions. I missed my dogs in Oman!

Dharamsala

We only taught one class a day, for an hour and a half, followed by a vegetarian lunch outside, so there was lots of time to explore in the afternoons. Dharamsala is the centre of learning for the Buddhist faith, and the bookstore had shelves full of books written by the Dalai Lama.

Dharamshala, (also spelled Daramsala,) is the winter capital of Himachal Pradesh Province in India, HP for short. Daramsala, 'Rest House for Pilgrims" is located in the scenic Kangra Valley surrounded by the majestic Deodar Cedar trees.

The Dalai Lama

The Dalai Lama, (Tenzin Gyatso), established the "Government in Exile" in Dharamsala in 1960, and the area has been the centre of the Tibetan exile world in India ever since. Today several thousand Tibetan exiles are settled in the area, and they have built monasteries, temples and schools promoting their faith and culture. The Namagyal Monastery, where his residence is located, had over 80, 000 manuscripts on Tibetan teachings. My neighbour, Dirk, a tech wizard, was in the process of putting these manuscripts online while I was there.

My Blessing

Whenever the Dalai Lama leaves his residence, his departure is announced by a police car driving ahead with its horns blaring. One morning, during our class, we heard the horns, and I excitedly told the students we were going to see the Dalai Lama! We hurried down the stairs, just as a police car came around the bend, and there he was in the second vehicle in the back seat! When he saw my foreign face he smiled his beautiful smile and blessed me by waving his arm over me through the window! It made my day!

My friend Brij was there too, but we thought he would easily be mistaken for one of the locals with his brown skin.

Naming a Child

I noticed that a lot of the Tibetan people had similar names. They have an interesting way of naming their children. The parents don't choose the names. Soon after a baby is born he or she is taken to the temple where one of the monks offers the mother or father a handful of names fanned out on pieces of paper. They choose one, and the name on that paper is the name of their child. All the names have been blessed by the Dalai Lama, so they are all good names. A lot of the male and female names, for example, Jigme, are the same.

Holi Festival

Holi, the festival of colors, was held in March soon after I arrived in India. The original meaning of the festival is good over evil, but as far as I could see it was an excuse to drink and throw colored powder over everyone. It was a lot of fun, and it was the first time I had ever had green hair. One of the dogs came with us, and this dog was sprinkled with pink powder. He attended my class for months afterwards waving his pink hindquarters.

Easter

I got into the habit of attending the Anglican church, St. John's in the Wilderness, which was aptly named, as it is in a grove of trees outside the city.

It must have been on a sightseeing itinerary. Often a bus would stop and the entire busload of people would walk in right up to the altar in the middle of the service!

I invited my colleagues to the Easter service, and we were all nationalities. We were asked to say Happy Easter in our own languages. There was English, German, Hindi, and Tibetan. Interesting! Most of the members were Indian nationals.

We then walked around the churchyard, where we saw many inscriptions, "Died in 1905", when the Kangra Valley suffered a major earthquake, which killed 20, 000 people. 1625 were from Dharamsala. The eighth earl Lord Elgin, Viceroy of India, died here and is buried at the cemetery. The inscription on his tomb says he died "After an encounter with a bear!"

Visa Run to Nepal- Cremations

As a Canadian, I was only allowed a three-month visa, and our contract was for five months, so I went to Nepal to renew it. I flew to Katmandu over the mountains and Pastor Chetti, an Indian pastor who I knew from Oman and was a missionary in Nepal, met my plane. He used to come from Muscat to preach at our church in Ibra. He took me and my large suitcase to my hotel on his motorbike!

My first afternoon there one of the desk clerks knocked on my door and asked me if I wanted to go for a walk. We crossed the dusty road, and we were suddenly on the banks of a sacred river, where cremations were being held, and prayers were being chanted.

Many people lined the riverbanks for these ceremonies. It was dusk, the time for cremations, and the air was full of smoke. The sky was a beautiful saffron colour. I felt as if I were in a movie.

Pokhara

Kathmandu is a big dusty city, with lots and lots of shopping opportunities, but I wanted to see more of Nepal.

When I was told my visa would not be ready for another ten days I made plans to go to Pokhara, a jewel of a city nestled in the mountains. I took the bus, which was a very bumpy ride for nine hours, and when we got close to Pokhara we passed the airport.

"That's how I'm going back," I said to myself, as it was only a one-hour flight. I didn't know what I was in for.

Pokhara, is known as the City of Lakes and Ponds, or Town of Mountain Ranges, because it is surrounded by snow- capped mountains and green hills. It is the second most populated city in Nepal after Kathmandu, located on the shore of beautiful Phewa Lake.

Near the Annapurna mountain range, three 8000 metre peaks can be seem from the city. I met a climber there, whose goal was to climb the highest mountains in the world.

Our computer teacher back in Dharamsala asked me to look up a Nepali lady who would be selling souvenirs near the lake. She was his mother-in-law. I had no trouble finding her with her large basket, and she invited me to dinner.

Her accommodation was very basic, with shared bathrooms for the tenants. She served me gyoza, or dumplings for dinner. These dumplings are claimed to be Chinese by the Chinese, Korean by the Koreans, and Japanese by the Japanese. Actually they originated in China. She left me in the living room alone for about half an hour, and when she returned she had a pair of shoes for her son-in-law for me to take with me.

Leaving Pokhara

After a few days in this idyllic place it was time to fly back to Kathmandu. I got to the airport early, and there were no lights on! I was told there was a storm, and that the airport was closed. I sat down and watched the cleaners washing the floor, and after about an hour the lights came on and I was able to check in for my flight.

This flight was even bumpier than the bus, and the girl in the seat next to me turned away from me. I thought she was very unfriendly, but as we were landing she told me she was "So scared."

Sir Edmund Hillary's wife and daughter were killed in a crash as they were leaving Kathmandu. It has a very short runway and is said to be one of the most dangerous airports in the world. But, visa in hand, I flew back to Dharamsala without incident.

My Birthday Celebration

Soon after I returned from Nepal it was time for my birthday, and my small room was full of people. Clifford brought the fireworks, Keldun brought the music, and the girls danced the night away. We had lots to eat and drink as well. It was one of the best birthdays I have ever had!

Paragliding

(Photo Credit Unsplash Peter Schultz)

Dharamsala is famous for its paragliding, and someone thought it would be fun to enjoy a flight. I wanted to try it, and I found out that I wouldn't be alone, and there would be someone steering the glider, so I signed up to go.

The day of the flight, we were scheduled to visit one of the local schools and do some other sightseeing. I just wanted to get it over with, but the school visit took a couple of hours. So, when we finally started up the mountain we were to jump off I was a bundle of nerves. It didn't help that Brij and Keldun spent the time chatting about the danger. It took half an hour to reach the top of the mountain, going around and around its base. Every turn around the mountain hid some of the sky, and the sound of my heart pounding was as loud as thunder!

When we got to the top we disembarked on a flat area and joined the other jumpers/flyers. I was given a parachute to climb into, and I went to join my friends to calm down. My partner called me a few minutes later, and when I heard my name my heart sank. He took control of the chute, which had a bar separating us, and I gripped it for dear life! I was told we had to run and jump, and the girl in front of us had to try twice before she was airborne. I was getting ready to leap into the air, but when I looked down, we were already there- in mid-air! Our balloon went straight up with a thermal, and I distracted myself by chatting with my instructor, asking him about his family and his job, etc.

About 15 minutes later we were going down over a series of rolling hills, and we could see the landing spot on the meadow below. I think we were in the air a total of half an hour. People were landing every-where, with big balloons strewn over the hillside, and I was worried about a crash landing. However, we landed smoothly, on grass. I shakily got to my feet and went with the others to celebrate with a tasty lunch.

Most of the time life wasn't as exciting as this, but I still enjoyed life in Mcleodganj where the charity was located. Sometimes we would take a bus to the Kotali Bazaar and the surrounding markets. I found an art store, and bought a simple book of paintings to copy and prac-tice my watercolour painting. I didn't have a TV or a laptop, so I would paint one picture a day, time permitting. I have never been artistic, but it's a learned skill, and I got better with practice.

The buses were very high off the ground and I had trouble getting in, but there was a man who pulled people onto the bus. At five feet ten I am not short, but what on earth did shorter people do? The seats were big enough to seat two people comfortably. Western people, that is. I was sitting with another lady, just getting settled, when two more women pushed onto the seat. It was a tight squeeze, but they were used to it, and I wasn't.

The Beggars

There were many beggars on the road up to Nyambal Temple, (The Dalai Lama's Temple.) Some of them were women carrying babies or small children. I saw one of them dump the child on the road when her shift was over. They would cry out for milk for the baby. We were warned not to buy any of this milk because they would just return it to the shops for money.

Dogs

Skinny, malnourished, dirty dogs were everywhere, and our charity would pick them up to spay and neuter them, and then release them back onto the street. The Dalai Lama agreed to allow suffering animals that were terminally ill to be euthanized. This was an exception to the Buddhist way of never killing any animal, because it could be resurrected as a human in the next life, but the director of our charity got special permission from him to do this so they wouldn't suffer.

Leaving Dharamsala

After five months our contract was finished. We had one more party to say goodbye to each other. They had good pizza in one place, an outdoor restaurant, but we couldn't hear each other speak because of the monkeys shaking the iron railings and shrieking at us. I think it was a territorial issue.

Goa

I had heard about Goa for years, and after my contract was over I decided to visit. It's a popular destination for backpackers and upscale visitors alike and is visited by a large number of tourists each year. Its white sand beaches, active nightlife, places to worship and its proximity to the Western Ghats rainforests, make it a popular place to visit at any time.

When I went it was rainy season, and many of the guest houses were closed, but I managed to find mine and check in. Even though it was the off season I still enjoyed the beautiful colonial houses everywhere.

I met a local girl who sold jewelry, and I bought a necklace from her that I still have, and took her to dinner. She was a struggling single mother like I had been for many years.

One scene that stands out in my memory was that of some fishermen early in the morning, about five or six, dragging their nets full of sardines onto the beach. A circle of seven or eight cows stood silently watching in the drizzling rain.

Ahmedabad

My friend in Oman, Franklin Christian, invited me to stay at his house in Ahmedabad. In Oman he lived a very simple life in one room, and walked everywhere, but-when he picked me up at the airport, he had a late model vehicle.

"Whose car is this, Franklin?"

And the beautiful house.

"Whose house is this, Franklin?"

The answer was "Mine!" to both questions.

I was given his father's room downstairs, and he went to stay with one of his other sons. He said he was "on vacation."

Anita, Franklin's beautiful wife, was very welcoming; so were his daughters. I was their honored guest. Anita, while working full time, still made delicious vegetarian meals. I think I put on a few pounds while I was there!

Ahmedabad is the most populous city in the Indian State of Gujarat. It was chosen by the Times of India to be India's best city to live in. It has become an important economic and industrial hub, listed in Forbes Magazine as one of the fastest growing cities of the decade. Compared to Canadian cities, its 8, 253, 000 population makes it the fifth most populous city in India, while Toronto, Canada's largest city is 6, 313, 000.

Gandhinagar

Gandhinagar, a mere 16 miles from Ahmedabad, is now the capital of Gujarat, and its claim to fame is that it is the birthplace of Mahatma Gandhi. We took a trip there and found a beautiful museum in Gandhi's honour with armed guards outside. But they told us it wouldn't be finished for another two years!

One day I went for a walk around the neighborhood, and looked up to see a family of monkeys sitting in a line on a stone wall with their tails neatly hanging down in a row.

Visakhapatnum

I was also invited to visit my friend Nicholas, an engineer in Visakhapatnum, so I got to see yet another interesting part of India. This city, also known as Vizag, or Waltair, is the largest and most populous city in the Indian state of Andhra Pradesh, located between the Eastern Ghats and the Coast of the Bay of Bengal.

Slums on the Beach

One evening we walked along the beach to a restaurant that Nicholas wanted to go to. This beach had slum villages right on the water, which is something I had never seen before. People were picking through hills of garbage close to the slums where they lived.

These were the poorest of the poor, but the kids who approached us had the biggest smiles I had ever seen! In most cases all they wanted was to be included in a photo. Nicholas had his camera and was ready to oblige them.

We saw areas of outdoor toilets- open air, and I had never seen that before either. The ladies, enveloped in voluminous saris, were shielded from prying eyes by their clothing. India has a lot of areas of "Open defecation" that are gradually being eliminated.

After about a week with Nicholas I wanted to visit friends in Hyderabad, but they told me they were busy at that time so I decided to let the internet decide my next destination. I prayed, and found an email from David, who said he was going to be in Bangkok for a few days. I bought a ticket to Bangkok. I really enjoyed my time in India, especially the food and the people, and hope I can visit again.

Back to Bangkok

I arrived at my hotel at 2 am- and the business centre was open! I sent an email to David to let him know where I was staying and I went upstairs to bed. I didn't have a phone number for him, and I didn't hear from him.

I spent the next day swimming and relaxing in my nice hotel, and when there was a tap on my door that evening I thought it was my order from room service. No, it was David, who had used several modes of transportation to get to my hotel that was very far from where he was staying, but close to the smaller airport, Don Moen. We had a nice visit for a couple of days and then went our separate ways.

Kathy and Joy

Kathy, an American woman married to a Thai, was renting out rooms in their second house as a retirement project. They lived close to the

Don Moen Airport where I landed and I moved into their place for a few days. She and her husband took me to the floating market. As residents they knew where a cheaper floating market was.

Kathy's husband Joy took care of the purchases so Kathy was able to shop unencumbered. There were lots of cheap things to buy at the floating market. We sat in long boats and were ferried up and down the canals. One friendly little boy on our boat asked me to buy him a gift. I refused, as it would probably be resold by his parents.

Chapter 9

Myanmar

Myanmar Memories

After a few months in Bangkok I found an ad for a job at a language school in Myanmar. The Director of Studies, Darren, was coming to Bangkok and we met in a restaurant in his hotel. He didn't offer me a job, but he invited me to Myanmar to "See the school."

Arrival in Myanmar

I flew there- a one-hour flight, and took a taxi to my hotel, on the golf course. It had a pool and I was looking forward to a dip. Then I realized it was raining, and the pool was full of algae. I met a man at breakfast the next morning who told me I was "in for a shock" as it was my first time in Myanmar. The morning traffic was horrendous, with people selling everything from newspapers to drinks and snacks to the long line of cars that was creeping along the highway.

Finally, I arrived at my school, and was invited to lunch by Shirley, the program director, so I "could experience Myanmar cuisine." I liked the fish.

The Decent Hotel

After lunch I was dropped at my hotel, with the bizarre name "Decent Hotel." Most of the taxi drivers didn't say it that way, and it sounded like "Decen Hotay" when they pronounced it. A lot of the countries in Southeast Asia "swallow" the final consonants of words.

The first day at the hotel I noticed something different. There was a lot of bumping and thumping from the room next door. I knew the maids had already cleaned the room, and then I thought, "Aha!" I realized the rooms were being rented by the hour as well as by the day.

I also noticed big welts in the creases of my body, which were sore and itchy. I took the hotel female owner, into the bathroom and showed them to her, and she laughed, a typical Asian reaction to feeling uncomfortable. But she got me a new, bug-free mattress. It was previously used by a Japanese guest, who told me that he and his wife broke up on their honeymoon! Better sooner than later!

A lot of the Myanmar people who lived on the cheaper upper floors would throw their garbage out the back window. These apartments were cheaper the higher they were, not more expensive like in the west. Most of these buildings had no elevators. This happened at my hotel, but it did have an elevator. I was glad I was on the opposite side of the building. A big flock of birds were usually picking through the pile of garbage below.

People would buy food and other things from the vendors on the street below by sending their money down in a wicker basket, which was attached to a long rope and would pull it up filled with the fruit, vegetables or whatever they wanted to buy. They would also send a key down for guests to get into the building, and I had one in my apartment, which was very useful!

The staff, mostly young women, were very nice, and even though they didn't speak a lot of English, were very kind to me.

My First Day

After a weekend sightseeing, (including the iconic Schwedegon Pagoda, the centre of the downtown core and the Buddhist faith, I arrived to observe a class at Nexus Language School. Well, the teacher I was supposed to observe didn't show up for class, so I offered to teach. We mostly reviewed the book they had been studying.

I didn't have to observe any more classes, and was given a contract. The students were mainly teenagers, and they were waiting for the time they would be placed in university, to study business, IT or Engineering.

I liked most of my classes except for one with seven girls. They came to class wearing heavy makeup, short skirts and false eyelashes, and told me they were working on their Master's in Business, which really surprised me, as they couldn't have dressed less businesslike. Every day they would filter in one at a time during the one hour and a half class. At least one student was absent in every class, and after a few weeks they decided to cancel the class, and I was relieved. I think they were moonlighting as bar girls.

My Class of Teenagers and Twenties

Local Dress

Both men and women dress in long, wrap- around skirts called Longyis. I did have a couple in my wardrobe, in fact one outfit was a gift from a student. But I was more comfortable in pants or dresses.

The students would usually be dressed in the blue and white uniforms they wore at the government schools they attended earlier in the day.

Socializing

I asked Darren, the DOS, about places to socialize in the area, and he suggested the Savoy Hotel. That night I got completely lost, and was about to dash across the busy street when a young boy standing next to me grabbed my hand and ran across with me! No words were exchanged, but I appreciated the help.

I finally did find the Savoy, a lovely colonial hotel where the expats hang out. I met the manager the first night. He was a young man, just having a beer with a friend. I became a regular at this hotel after a few weeks, and also enjoyed visiting the 50th St Bar where they had excellent pizza, and also Trivia Nights. David and I went to one when he came to visit. Another popular place was the iconic Strand Hotel downtown near the waterfront. They had a Happy Hour every Friday, and the tasty snacks were free with the drinks. I also enjoyed the Pansodan Gallery, that had a Happy Hour every Tuesday evening, This was a large art gallery where local artists' work was displayed. The owner would treat foreigners and locals alike to his delicious soups and stews.

David and Mary.

In Bangkok I was referred to a man in Myanmar called "O.J." Not the famous football player, but a man who was working to translate the bible into the Burmese language. We met once, and he called me back a few days later to give me the names and numbers of a British couple who were working at a local seminary. He said, "They are your age." Some people don't care about this and some do.

Mary and I would meet on Fridays and check out the local galleries, and one memorable evening we attended a concert with some performers from Ireland playing the Celtic harp, and also local performers playing the Burmese harp, a round instrument. There was a lot of goodwill that evening between the two cultures playing

Baby in Bath on a Trip With Mary

together, and officials from both countries presiding. They told us the Burmese instrument was very complicated and difficult to play.

Transportation around town was always in taxis, but the air-conditioned ones were more expensive. Most of the time I was on my own, except when my friend Barbara came to visit, and David came for a few days as well, and enjoyed making videos of the street life.

The Hindu Festival – Self Inflicted torture!

Our hotel was next to an open-air market. The dogs would sit patiently waiting for the butchers to throw them a scrap of meat. I would buy fruit there and it was a great place to people-watch.

One day I was at the market and could hear some loud music coming from the next street. The entire area had been transformed into a festival. There was carpeting on the ground, banners, music, food and young men impaling themselves on needles. One of them, with needles sticking out of his chest, looked at me with a sad smile. In spite of the needles he didn't look like he was in pain. These festivals honour the Lord Shiva, who gives them strength and courage. Hindus believe their crops will fail without this show of devotion. Sometimes this extreme piercing involves spears, axes and hooks. I was glad I didn't witness this.

The Dogs

Stray dogs were everywhere, especially during mating season. Watching them copulate was not a pretty sight, as they would get stuck together, and it was hard to separate them. It was sad, because it meant more and more puppies would be born. Starving, they would savagely fight for a crust of bread. I decided to count the puppies on my way to work one day. There were fourteen! This was within a three block radius!

Some of them would hide under cars during the day as it was cooler for them. Then – they were all gone! I asked someone where they were and they told me that they had all been run over by the cars!

Another litter was born soon after that, the puppies would get stuck in the double doors of the school and would interfere with anyone trying to get in and out. One day they all disappeared. I was told a woman had come and taken them all away in a car. To adopt them?

Stray dog with pups

I found one pitiful looking bitch in the market, with one eye weeping yellow pus, and a huge lump on her face. I managed to persuade a vet to come and see her and he said she had cancer and had had it for a long time. He was going to take her back to his office, and one of the ladies from the market walked ahead luring her with a chicken foot. We went a few blocks when suddenly there was an explosion of barking from an enormous black dog so we retreated back to the market to avoid him.

I went back to the market to bathe her eye a few more times, and she always licked my hand in gratitude. Then one day she was gone. I asked a woman (with sign language,) and she said she had died. A blessing, I think.

My Business Class –
Workers from the Cigarette Factory

I was assigned an adult class of workers from the nearby cigarette factory. They said they went to work by ferry, but there was no body of water around, and I learned they came by the company mini-van. They said it was a good place to work and the newest employee had been there for seven years!

I was told to take off my shoes to go to their classroom. I didn't want to, because the floor wasn't too clean, and it was uneven linoleum, but as a good employee I complied. I was running around the classroom one morning with a handout for our lesson when I slipped and fell on the uneven floor. I just sat there for a few minutes, and one of the men in the class rushed to my side and started gently massaging my foot. I got a laugh when I asked him if he was married. After a few minutes I got up and we continued our class. I didn't know the fall had weakened my foot and I would spend a month in a cast!

On one of my walks around the city I thought to myself that it was only a matter of time before I broke a bone on the uneven pavement. The paving blocks were large, but not secure, and sometimes I would step on one and it would lean to one side or another. It was like walking up a see-saw.

Spring Festival Fracture

It was the Chinese holiday Spring Festival, and I saw that there would be a Lion Dance across from my favourite hotel, the Savoy. It was supposed to start at 9 pm, and I went in for a glass of wine before the dance began. There were hordes of people on the street and sidewalks. It was a busy weekend evening and everyone was out. The Lion Dance was just ending, and the "Lions" on the back of a truck were deflated. I must have slipped on some water on the street, and suddenly I was DOWN and couldn't move.

People were pulling my arms trying to help me up. I was unable to get up for a few minutes. We were outside a disco and the manager appeared and offered me a ride. He kindly asked if I wanted to go to the hospital or my hotel. I said I would be okay in the morning, so he dropped me at the hotel. I went straight to bed, but in the morning when I tried to put weight on my foot there was a shooting pain in my foot and leg. I had to drag myself to the bathroom using a broom handle.

I called Darren and told him what had happened and he said he would send one of the girls from the office to help me. He would have come himself but he had a student coming to his house. Shortly after this Margaret, the sweetest one of the girls arrived, and took me to the hospital for an x-ray. I was helped into a wheelchair, and we had to go to another building across a busy street (they were all busy), and the orderly didn't put the brakes on when we had to stop. I felt unsafe sitting there with the traffic zooming by.

I liked the doctor, though, and he had a daughter in our school. He told me I had a small fracture in my ankle- the same foot I had hurt in the classroom. He said that I would have to wear a cast for a month, so we stopped at a store so I could get some crutches. I couldn't walk, so Margaret went in and bought the longest crutches she could find, which turned out to be too long. I had to go back the next day to get a cast from my ankle to my knee.

I had a class that day, and the girls all squeezed into my small room with some of them sitting on my bed. Dina, my Bosnian student, had brought me lunch, which was much appreciated. I didn't miss any classes at all.

When I was more mobile I was able to take a taxi to the school a few blocks away.

The girls working at my hotel were very kind and thoughtful. Every morning two of them would come to my room and help me take a shower with my leg wrapped in plastic.

And about five pm every day, one of them would knock on my door and say,

"Go outside?" I would lean on her shoulder, which was much lower than mine, and we would go through the market and around the neighborhood, with the local people asking: "What's wrong with her leg?"

They have the same word for leg and foot in their language.

I took these girls out for some special meals to thank them, and I think they enjoyed themselves, but I had to bring someone else along to translate.

Dinner Out

I was invited to dinner by a woman from the States who was given my email by her pool man who I had met in Chiang Mai. We were to meet at a fancy hotel. But a wedding party was in progress, and the ramp I needed to use with my wheelchair was part of the wedding tableau. The staff at the hotel- I think four guys- just grabbed my chair and lifted me up a flight of stairs! Scary but exciting!

Getting My Cast Off

The month went quickly and soon it was the time to get my cast off!

The doctor put a very narrow piece of metal along my leg, and then cut off the cast.

"Goodbye!" He said. "Call us if you have a problem!"

After I got home I called one of my students, who a physiotherapist. She was shocked.

"You mean you weren't given any exercises to do?"

She came over to my room right away with a sheet full of exercises to strengthen my ankle, and referred me to her professor, a physio at a nearby hospital. It catered mostly to locals, and there was very little English spoken there. The doctor did speak English, and he was a great help. My student also taught me how to use my crutches as nobody had shown me. Even though they were too long for me, I made do.

My New Apartment

After six months at the Decent Hotel I wanted to get my own place, but housing was a problem. I went to look at about half a dozen apartments, but the landlords wanted payment for a full year in advance, and none of them were furnished, which was another expense.

Luckily, one of the guys at work was subletting his apartment in the middle of Chinatown. It would be further to go to work, and it was a more interesting area. I went to see it and I was impressed with the furniture, hardwood floors and two bedrooms. There were stairs to climb, but I had recovered enough to climb up the three flights. I still had to use the crutches until my muscles warmed up in the morning.

The Cleaning Lady

The day I moved in a local lady showed up to clean. She was sent by the girlfriend of the guy I was renting from, and she came weekly from that time on. She did a wonderful job. She even brought me flowers, every week!

Living in Chinatown

It was fun to go shopping for vegetables at 7 am, and see the ladies sitting cross-legged on plastic sheets ready to sell. They must have been up for hours. One lady always smiled and said hello. Everything was cheap and very fresh, and it was good to be able to cook again.

I always took a taxi to my school. One day my driver rear-ended the one in front of him. Only slight damage, and we were on our way again soon. One of them told me the police used to get into their taxi, ask how much money they had and demand they give it to them.

The Military

Men in army uniforms were everywhere, and the titles at the bookstore were mostly military as well. In Cambodia, I met Douglas, the Burmese manager of FCC Hotel, and I asked him which country he preferred.

His answer, "Well, in Cambodia you can go anywhere."

Cell Phones

When I first arrived in Myanmar cell phones were ridiculously expensive, with one costing between $1500 USD and $2000 USD. They were bequeathed to family members in their wills. Needless to say I didn't buy one.

When we got paid, it was half in the local currency, khat, and half in US dollars. We were given a shopping bag to carry the money which was in small denominations. This changed during my stay of a year and a half, when we were given the money in larger denominations. The cell phones dropped in price, and David was able to get a cheap one when he came to visit., but the reception was terrible.

Bangkok Breaks

Our school had a lot of connections, and had interests in many businesses—Not just education. "A Finger in Every Pie." They sent us to Bangkok every ten weeks to renew our visas which were all business visas. One of these visa runs was when I was still on crutches, so I was pushed to the front of the line in a wheelchair. This was great, as the lines are always long in airports. I wondered how they were going to take my picture as I was not within its range; but then I saw it had a swivel and could take photos anywhere!

Darren told me if I had any other health problems to go directly to Bangkok, as the medical care in Myanmar was not nearly as good.

Yangon Hospital

Darren himself became very ill, and went to the cleanest, newest hospital in Yangon. He was given a bill for $2000 USD for his weekend visit, and he was still ill, with what they suspected was a Deep Vein Thrombosis. This is a blood clot in a vein which can block arteries to the heart, so could be a life-threatening condition. He was transferred in a screaming ambulance to Yangon Hospital, which was an old copper-coloured set of buildings very close to my apartment. A lot of people in Myanmar don't pull over and stop for ambulances, even with the sirens blaring! Darren remarked that he could have died just because someone was in a hurry to go to lunch! Darren was immediately put into the ICU department, on a heart monitor, and started to improve right away.

The outside corridors were lined with rusty railings, and sleeping families were everywhere. They spread their longyis on the floor for bedding and many of them were nursing their babies. A lot of them came from other provinces and couldn't afford a hotel, so they slept at the hospital wherever they could find room. Small children were there as well, and street vendors looked after their needs.

At the time I had a recurring gastric problem, and it got so when I showed up at the emergency apartment the man in charge would shout gasroenteritus! I went there a few times, but the problem would always come back, and the last time I was there I stayed overnight on the emergency ward.

The beds were all out in the open, so I was able to see the patients being brought in. One man came in with his skin a dark blue colour. I was told he was badly burned. On one of my many trips to the bathroom that night I encountered a stray dog in the hallway. We passed each other and I wondered what he was doing there. The doors were wide open and there was no security that late at night. I think he was looking for food or companionship.

The next morning I saw a doctor who referred me to a clinic the foreigners used, and the diagnosis was a parasite. The female doctor at that clinic told me she bought mohinga, the popular fish soup in the open-air market, but she boiled it on the stove for at least 15 minutes before she served it to her family.

My problem cleared up in a few days with medication, and Darren was up and back to work in a few weeks.

I read about this hospital in the local paper. I was shocked to see the headline:

"Man shot in the heart survives!"

I was joyfully amazed!

The hospital has a reputation for having good doctors. It was an example of not judging a book by its cover.

Back to Bangkok

When my contract in Yangon was finished I headed back to Bangkok to look for work.

I only stayed in Bangkok for a few months, with a one-month diversion in Chiang Mai, and even though I had friends there it was a lonely time. But it was good to be back in a modern city with all the conveniences. Yangon didn't even have a Mcdonald's.

Bangkok is a city of ten million people including the surrounding areas. It's a shoppers' paradise, with goods to accommodate every budget. This fast-paced city has trains, overpasses, luxury hotels, and first class medical care. When I was living in Cambodia I had to have a complete medical for health insurance, and I went to the Bangkok Hospital. I had so many tests that I took a book to read, but every time I sat down after yet another test, I think there were 25 of them—someone would be in my face asking my name and taking me to the next one. I was completely exhausted.

My Teaching

I was able to secure a part time teaching job: one-on-one teaching with students from nearby Chulalongkorn University. It took two trains to get to my teaching job, and I got an age-related discount on one of them. Bangkok is a very busy place with an excellent transportation system, and I would always pick up a take-away breakfast of mango and sticky rice-delicious!

One thing I enjoyed was the many "Meet Ups." These were for any age group or taste and varied from church services to hiking. I joined a Toastmaster's club. We went for dinner after the meetings, which were a lot of fun.

First Trip to Cambodia

On Khosan Road, the famous road through the tourist area of Bangkok, I saw a van with a big colorful sign advertising "Trip to Cambodia" Only $200 US! This included the hotel, meals and the visa, so I signed up to go. All went well until we arrived at the border, and then we had to get on a larger bus that was packed with people. There were no seats for the company staff, and one man asked if he could sit on my sandal, as he was getting hot from sitting over the engine. I agreed, but once we arrived in Siem Reap, "Templetown" we were dumped off outside the city, and I complained about paying extra to get to the hotel. I thought all the transportation was included. The same guy who had borrowed my sandal, then threw my luggage down onto the ground. Everyone was hot, tired and grouchy as we had been travelling for about 8 hours including the wait at the border.

I had to pay extra for the aircon in the hotel but the meals were included. Some of my fellow passengers had been there before and went to the hotels they liked. Ours was on a dirt road, and was a run-down place. I stayed there but should have moved to a better place.

I did go to the famous Angkor Wat Temples, and enjoyed my time there, especially Bayon Temple, the temples with stone faces etched onto them. I was impressed with my tuk-tuk driver, who was studying tourism at university. It was a very bright sunny day, and I was constantly putting on and then taking off my sunglasses. After one trip inside I realized I didn't have the glasses, and quickly went back to check. No glasses. This also happened when I was shopping one day. I missed the glasses immediately, but when I went inside two minutes later the people in the store said they hadn't seen them. Yeah, right!

Chapter 10

Moving to Cambodia

Cambodia Overview

Cambodia, officially the Kingdom of Cambodia, is a country located in the southern part of the Indochinese Peninsula. It is bordered by Thailand to the northwest, Laos to the north, Vietnam to the east, and the Gulf of Thailand to the southwest.

Its population is over 17 million, and Buddhism is the official state religion, with over 97% of the inhabitants practising that religion, the same as Myanmar. Minority groups include Vietnamese, Chinese, and over 30 hill tribes.

Cambodia has a tropical monsoon climate of two seasons, dry and rainy. For those of us from North America the heat and humidity can be oppressive, with no winter to speak of. Temperatures range from 21c to 35c, during the hottest month in April.

I spent four years in Cambodia; two in Siem Reap and the other two in Phnom Penh, the capital city, which is the political, economic and cultural centre of Cambodia.

Life in Seam Reap

Siem Reap [siəm riəp]) is the second-largest city of Cambodia, as well as the capital and largest city of Siem Reap Province in northwestern

Cambodia. It's known as "The City of Temples" named after the famous Angkor Wat, Cambodia's most famous tourist attraction.

With its awe-inspiring temples, colorful cafes, and placid waterways, Siem Reap is a jewel of Southeast Asia. French Colonial and Chinese-style architecture in the Old French Quarter and around the Old Market lend the city an old-world ambiance. Some of the buildings have been made into hotels and shops and restaurants. Courtesy Wikepedia

One of David's first gigs -singing and guitar playing was at the Central Café near the river and the Old Market. I used to enjoy strolling along the river, especially around Christmastime when the hotels are decorated in tiny stars.

In the city, there are museums, traditional Apsara dances and a varied and interesting night life. Siem Reap today being a popular tourist destination-has many hotels, resorts, and restaurants. The streets are full of Chinese, Vietnamese, and Western tourists from the USA and every European country. The city has just been refurbished, as of 2021, and streets are wider and cleaner than before. Of course the friendly smiles of the local people are an added attraction. Most of the tuk-tuk drivers speak English, and the hotel name cards are bilingual.

Credit Wikipedia

Thousands of people visit the site, spend three days in Siem Reap and leave. It's a must see for any visitors to the area. Before the pandemic, 2.6 million foreign visitors came to the site yearly, but attendance plummeted to 200,000 in 2021. Foreigners pay an entrance fee, but locals and their families are free. A lot of them often go to the site and enjoy a picnic on the grass in front of the huge edifice.

These temples comprise the largest religious monument in the world, on 400 acres of land. The largest, with the pineapple shaped towers was originally constructed as a Hindu temple dedicated to the god Vishnu by King Suryavarman 11, and it was gradually transformed into a Buddhist temple towards the end of the 12th Century. Angkor Wat is one of the most important pilgrimage sites for Buddhists in Cambodia and around the world. Their intricate carvings tell stories of war, and are a valuable record of historical events, because no other writings existed at the time.

These temples are proudly displayed on the Cambodian flag, and a six-kilometre moat encircles them. The temples cover a vast area. A lot of people rise early to catch the sun rising over the temples at 5 am, but the morning we went the sky was cloudy.

Moving to Cambodia

After a few months in Thailand I decided to try my luck in Cambodia. David had moved there a year previously and I went to spend some time with him and his Chinese family, who were visiting for a few days. It was just a one-hour flight, and I stayed in a boutique hotel with David and his family. There was a pool there and we all enjoyed the water, especially the baby, Cici.

One morning I took a tuk-tuk down dusty High School Road, where a lot of the schools were located, and dropped off some resumes. They all seemed interested in hiring me at $10 an hour. I had been warned about this by Mike, a colleague in Myanmar, but it was a bit of a shock after the comfortable salary I was getting in Oman.

I was hired by the University of South East Asia, and rented an apartment nearby with a swimming pool! My landlord was a charming Frenchman, with a Cambodian wife and two bright sons, one in grade two and the other one studying four languages: English, Khmer, the Cambodian language, French and Spanish. I tried speaking French with him (I used to get prizes for this language years ago), but he told me my French was "terrible."

I was also hired by Pannasastra University, pronounced "Panyasa" by the locals. Our contracts were only for one semester, or three months, usually for only half a day. Most of us had other jobs elsewhere. My colleagues were local Cambodians, (Khmers), British, American and Canadian. I became friends with Miriam, a Filipina teacher. We used to go to the local restaurants for dinner after class.

Our classes ran from 3:30 in the afternoon until 7:30 at night. These students came to us after their regular classes in local schools. A lot of them rushed from one school to another, and some would come flying in late. After class it was a busy, noisy time on the road, with 500 students revving their motorbikes.

An Uninvited Guest

During the rainy season, a lot of bugs and lizards would seek shelter inside. One of my classes was a very unruly class of twelve year-olds, and one night the noise level was higher than usual. One of the boys pointed to a very large gecko on the wall. It was facing downwards; frozen in fear. I called the maintenance man. He came quickly and hit the lizard with a broom and it fell onto the floor and then ran around the perimeter of the classroom. The students were screaming and the noise was deafening!

The man finally caught it by the tail and took it outside, holding its mouth open like a captured snake, and when I asked him what he did with it he said he released it outside.

Another Uninvited Guest

One night David and I were having dinner at the Palm Restaurant, a place with low walls that didn't go all the way to the ceiling. It was raining outside. Suddenly, something fell from the roof onto a beam and then onto my plate! Luckily I had finished eating! It was a huge scorpion-like creature, about six inches long. Some kind of cockroach, I think. I was doing a crossword from the newspaper, and its tail landed there. Maybe it wanted to improve its English?

A Cambodian Wedding

One of the interesting things about teaching overseas was learning about the cultural differences. When one of the school directors invited me to his wedding I asked him how many people would be attending the event.

He answered, "One thousand." I was really surprised and thought the venue would be a hotel with a conference room to accommodate so many people, but I just didn't understand weddings in Khmer (pronounced K-mai) culture.

The people I was going with didn't seem worried about the time, and when we finally arrived there after waiting for a couple of hours for the girls to get ready, we saw a group of people leaving! After depositing our money for the bride and groom under the watchful eyes of the mothers-in-law, we were escorted to a round table. There is a set price for the tables, so they try to fill them up to seat eight. Drinks, beer and fruit drinks were brought in plastic baskets, then the meal was served. After we finished there was a lot of toasting, with people visiting other tables to toast the other guests.

The bride and groom were wearing colourful outfits, which they changed every few hours. Loud music was playing, which is something that happens at all special occasions in Cambodia, and we all moved in a giant wheel in time to the music.

After about an hour we were escorted out, and met new groups entering as we were leaving. I finally understood how they could accommodate so many people!

David and Me at Tuk Tuk Tacos

Air Conditioning

We had air conditioners, but they were not always working in Cambodia. As in China, another poor country, the power is often sold to other countries. Someone would "get word" that the power would be out the next day. A lot of hotels were exempt from this, so a lot of us would get a hotel room for the day- $15-$20 USD and relax in the pool or the room in air-conditioned comfort.

Dr. Beat Richner

A few days after I arrived in Siem Reap I picked up a brochure advertising a free cello concert, so that evening I rode in a tuk-tuk to the hospital where it was being held. "Beaticello" was the title of the concert. The cellist was a Dr. Beat Richner, from Switzerland, and he entertained us with music, a video presentation and the story of his hospitals.

He had come to Cambodia as a young pediatrician, with a heart for the Cambodian people and their children. He raised enough money to build a hospital, then another one and another until there were five, in Siem Reap and Phnom Penh. He would fly there every week with his "silent partner", his cello, on the seat beside him. The flight attendant teased him about his silent seatmate.

Dr. Richner devoted his whole life to Cambodian children, and saved a lot of lives over the years. He used a lot of humour in his presentation, and also wrote books for sale of course. I bought one and was very impressed with his dedication. I met him in person a couple of times, as he used to have breakfast in the next restaurant to mine. He was very gracious, and thanked me for my donation.

Sadly, a few months later I heard that he went back to Switzerland in poor health, and passed away a few weeks later. He was in his early 70's.

David

One advantage to living in Siem Reap was I was able to go and listen to my son David sing at the bars and restaurants around town. He was the headliner at FCC, or the Foreign Correspondent's Club, an upscale hotel, where he played and sang in the open-air dining room.

Sometimes I was the only guest, but I still enjoyed the ambiance and the food.

Love You Restaurant

"We came up with the idea of opening a restaurant. Shareholders were students. They were not Siem Reap residents. They were from a floating village located in one province of Cambodia. One of them was an orphan. Another one was a school security guard. Every day they worked, ate and slept at the restaurant. We sold food and drink at the minimum price that customers could afford. We were so friendly. We took care all customers. Food and drinks were so delicious."

(They were!) Those things help encourage more customers to come and support us. (We did, and for a while it was the "In" place to go!)

Written by Hen Sodet, teacher, entrepreneur and friend

Sodet and Me at Love You!

Friends in Siem Reap

I made friends among the expat community and also among the locals. Age didn't seem to matter. I reached out to the Christian community, and soon connected with a ladies' bible study group. There were Americans in the group, and ladies from Taiwan, Japan, Australia and New Zealand. It was fun being part of an international group, and while we have gone our separate ways, it's fun to keep in touch on Facebook. Minako, a Japanese Canadian, still does a ministry in Cambodia with her husband, and Anne still hosts the bible study group. Another member, Glenys, has just published her memoir. She started a ministry for poor women, called Women of Worth. They learned how to sew and create beautiful handbags and other souvenirs. These ladies have now become independent businesswomen, and one of them was able to install electricity in her house for the first time.

The Hair Salon

An Australian girl in the group recommended a hairdresser in a local market, and she said this was the only person she would trust to do her hair. The woman could speak a little English and I went for a hair cut and colour every few months. I was directed to a red plastic sofa, where the ladies and a sometimes men would lie down, Cambodian style. Being tall I had to put my feet on the wall, but it was very cheap and they did a good job. A relaxing head massage was included in the price.

It was a very basic salon, with the little girl playing on the floor and the perfume of raw fish wafting in from the wet market next door.

Louise

The pastor at the church, Ivor, asked me to befriend a lady who was being transferred to Siem Reap from Battambang, another province. She was being discharged from the hospital, where she was supposed to undergo surgery for her hip, but it turned out she wasn't strong enough to undergo the surgery.

Ivor thought we might "become friends" because we were about the same age and were both Canadian. I used to visit her on a weekly basis. I enjoyed the ride by tuk tuk out to the countryside. My driver, Savy, only charged me $5.00 for these trips, and he was a great help with Louise who was bedridden. She had mental problems, so it wasn't always easy to visit her.

I went to visit her many times, and the last time I saw her she was in a hospital in Phnom Penh. She had to have an x-ray to see if she could go ahead with the surgery. They picked her up in a blanket and ran down the stairs with her! She was on her way back to Canada.

The Night Market

Every kind of food, music, souvenirs, and clothing are available at the Night Market.

A woman with a big bamboo platter came along to offer fresh cockroaches. I think they were fried. I didn't partake of this delicacy, but I did try a meal worm, and it was tasty.

The Bugs Cafe

The Bugs Café was a very popular place with tourists, and I saw a big crowd there one night. I went in and was about to try one of their dishes, but when I saw the tarantula stuffed into the samosa I changed my mind.

Here are some of the unique offerings at the Bugs Cafe:

"Bug Mac" – burger with insect steak, sweet potato fries, home-made bread

"Savoury cupcakes" – olive and parmesan cupcakes garnished with crickets and silkworms

"Tarantula donuts" – whole marinated tarantulas coated in tempura and deep fried

"Pan fried scorpions" – marinated scorpions with garlic, parsley and cashew nuts

Unfortunately this restaurant has closed permanently since the Pandemic, but I am sure similar food can be found for the asking. Bugs and grubs are very popular snacks with Cambodians and tourists alike.

The Food!

A lot of the food is very reasonably priced, and a meal can be enjoyed for as little as $2.00 or $3.00 USD. Street food is everywhere, and restaurants to accommodate all budgets are available. One of my favourites was **Jungle Burger**. With its jungle motif and New Zealand owner, It was a fun place to go. I met a Canadian couple there on their honeymoon! The burgers and chicken dishes are very tasty. Fresh fruits and juices are available, and tasty entrees and desserts made with coconut.

A popular breakfast is grilled pork on rice with fried egg on top, with pickles, soup and sweet chili , for dipping or pouring. The meals were always beautifully presented, and my friend Miriam always took photos of her meals before eating.

She had promised to join me to help me celebrate my 70th birthday by going ziplining for the day. It was something I had wanted to try for a long time.

We were to meet at a hotel, but she didn't answer my many calls that morning. She told me later that she had to go and help some visitors and it was a chance to make some extra money. No apology.

The Flight of the Gibbon: My 70th Birthday!

When she saw I was alone, a friendly woman from Calgary hung out with me for the day. Her company was much appreciated. A doctor, she was travelling with her two daughters. One of them gave birth to the ziplining adventure.

The Flight of the Gibbon was the former name of the zipline company. Maybe this was because there were no gibbons to be seen. They did take good care of our little group of ten, and were known for their high standards of safety. We were strapped into harnesses, which were then either hooked onto the long cable that we travelled along or one of the ten trees we flew between.

We had a short trial run, just a few metres long, just to see if there were any serious problems with the group. We sat in little baskets suspended in the air, and one of the workers would give us a little push. Then off we went flying through the air at a high speed and then were caught at the other end by another worker. We were not allowed to hook or unhook the cables ourselves.

At first we were all nervous. "After you!" and "No, it's your turn!" was heard a lot. Then, after the first five sections of our route, where we had to walk across a wooden bridge with big gaps between the slats, everyone started to relax.

Instead of hanging on to the safety bar for dear life, we would raise our hands in the air and shout "Woohoo!"

The last five sections were a piece of cake, but I started to worry about how we would get down to the forest floor. Again, there was nothing to worry about as we were well -protected all the way. After sliding down to the ground though a storm suddenly came up, and the strong wind was even blowing branches around. If we had descended five minutes later we might have been in trouble.

We had a short nature walk and then arrived safely back to the restaurant for a delicious lunch. But if we were still up in the trees, on our cables, in a windstorm, it might have been a different story.

Leaving Siem Reap

It had always been my plan to move to Phnom Penh if I wanted a change from the touristy town of Siem Reap. ACE (Australian Centre for Education) had a school in Siem Reap, and one day I was passing by that school, saw decorations and heard music playing and met a nice blonde man who was sweeping the entranceway. They were having an open house. When I told him I was a teacher he invited me in to "Have a chat." I don't have the CELTA qualification that most of the ACE teachers have, but I have other credentials. Like my online Master's in English. He said he would send it the HR director,

Nakrisakpeak. A lot of Cambodians have long names like this, and many of them use nicknames.

A short time later ACE advertised for teachers, and so I applied again. This time I received an email from Nakrisakpeak, and he wanted to do a Skype interview. I asked if the job was in Siem Reap or Phnom Penh. He said Phnom Penh, and it paid $5.00 more an hour than in Siem Reap.

I didn't have a computer, and the internet café I used was a very noisy place the day of my Skype interview. There was a thunderstorm, and rain was falling on the metal roof. I felt relaxed during the interview, and thought I might have a chance of getting the job. Sure enough, I received an email to say that if my references were verified they would hire me for the next month of July.

Chapter 11

Phnom Penh

Phnom Penh is the biggest and wealthiest city in Cambodia, and its population is almost three million. There is a lot more hustle and bustle than in Siem Reap, and it has been described as "Ramped up Siem Reap." There are more shopping malls, more restaurants and more schools. There are also markets for clothing, shoes, and souvenirs.

My friend Jackie was wearing a beautiful dress one day and I asked her about it. They were six dollars each, so she bought one for every day of the week! Those same dresses would be over $100 here in Canada.

The city sits at the junction of the Tonle Sap and the mighty Mekong River, that has its source in former Tibet. Riverboats travel up and down the river. When David was visiting we went on a tour boat with a beautiful meal. We were with a group, and tickets were by donation and seconds were available. I think David had three helpings!

Phnom Penh was a hub for both the Khmer Empire and the French Colonialists. French baguettes are found in food stalls with Khmer Cuisine. As in Siem Reap, beautiful colonial houses have been converted into embassies and restaurants.

A wide walking area skirts the waterfront, which is lined with parks and restaurants. The Silver Pagoda, The National Museum and the Royal Palace are all in that area, and for a price of ten US Dollars each they are open to tourists.

Phnom Penh is also the home of Hun Sen, the prime minister, who has held this position for over 35 years. When I was there he dissolved the major opposition party, and its leaders were exiled to France and other places. I read a book entitled "Life Under Hun Sen." It was an eye-opener!

Moving to Phnom Penh

I wasn't offered a free airplane ticket, so I took a taxi all the way to Phnom Penh. The driver spent all of his time calling and catching up with his friends. The cost was $60 USD, and I was able to take some of my household goods with me.

My friend Sandy had recommended the Frangipani Hotel, and the cost included breakfast, a beautiful pool and spacious room. It was expensive though and very far from the school where I would be teaching. I only stayed there a few days.

Milo and Me in our new place

My New Apartment

I was telling one of the desk clerks about my new job, and he offered to help me find an apartment close to my campus. After a day of training I had come back and sank into the relaxing blue pool. The clerk said he had made an appointment to see the apartment, so I reluctantly got out of the water and dressed quickly.

After getting ready we set out, and I mentioned something about drivers getting lost.

He said, "Don't worry. I won't get lost."

It was very hot and crowded on the roads, and we drove around the same area for an hour. He made a lot of calls. We were lost.

We finally found the place, and the apartment was lovely. Just one bedroom, but very spacious. And the rent included cleaning three times a week.

Canada Day

I moved to Phnom Penh on July 1, Canada Day, and found a place that was advertising a Canada Day celebration. It was a long ride on the tuk-tuk, and I didn't know my way around the city at all, but I was happy to be able to celebrate our national day. I didn't meet many Canadians in Cambodia, and my co-workers were Khmer, British, American, and lots of Australians.

Our First Day: Christmas in July!

The first day of our training I called from the taxi to confirm the location. Sure enough the driver had to make a u-turn and drive to another area! The main campus was in another part of town from where I would be teaching. When I breathlessly rushed into the room I was met with silence. The room was full, and there were a couple of guys making a welcome speech.

They were the same two who had interviewed me, and one of them was Naprisakpeak! I was happy when he told us his nickname was Kim! The other one was Aaron Kelly, who was the DOS. They were wearing welcoming smiles, and we were made to feel part of the team. Our photos were taken, and we were given some high quality gifts! One of them was a motorbike helmet, and I promptly gave it to my friend Sodet, who needed one more than I did. We had a delicious buffet lunch, and everyone was in a happy mood.

After lunch we all piled into a car to go to our campus, Santhor Mok, and meet our new director. ACE doesn't provide elevators for teachers or students, but I soon got used to the stairs. One thing I really liked was having my own desk! I had worked so many places where I didn't have my own personal space and I really appreciated it.

I didn't know that after the "renovations" we would be using lockers for our things and that our personal space would be a thing of the past.

We started training the next day. I was given a level 8 class, which was elementary. The students had as much personality as a block of wood! They did improve as time went on, but they were not nearly as lively as I was used to.

The Dogs

My new apartment had a half wall in the basement and it was easy for anyone to break in and steal things in the basement. After this happened a few times the owners decided to get some guard dogs to keep intruders away.

A few days after I moved into my new place I noticed three dogs in the basement. Two of them were black and the third was a rusty colour. She had a round belly and I wondered if she was pregnant. I found out a couple of weeks later. Lyda, the female, was lying in a comfortable place under the stairs licking her hind quarters. She gave birth to six puppies over the next few hours.

They were tiny little balls of grey fluff, scratching for a place of nourishment. They all had flat faces. But, when I came back from a month's vacation they all had long noses, and looked very different. While she was nursing Lyda looked worn out and haggard, and very thin. I was worried about her, but as soon as she stopped nursing she regained her normal weight and looked healthy again.

Milo and Rocky

From an early age, Milo and his brother Rocky took a liking to me, and would follow me around. One night I came home from work, took the elevator to my third floor apartment, and there were Milo and Rocky waiting for me on the mat outside my door! Most of the time they would come to my place and wrestle, as puppies do. I rarely gave them food, but I did take them to the vet for their vaccinations. Both dogs had a condition called cryptorchidism. Milo had both testicles inside his body, and Rocky had one inside and one outside. The vet said, nonchalantly, "They could die." Surgery was expensive so I did nothing for a few months. But one afternoon, Rocky came into my apartment and started systematically spraying the furniture! Horrified, I called the vet, who said, "We have free surgery on Monday. Bring them in then."

I did take them in, with the help of one of the guys who worked in the basement. The clinic was a long way from my apartment, and we went in the hottest part of the day, and got lost. We finally made it, and the vet told me I would have to pick them up that night, as they didn't keep animals overnight. It was a long, busy day, with teaching in between, but I made it back to pick up the two dogs. They were still very lethargic after the surgery, so I took them upstairs to sleep at my place. They woke up in the middle of the night and were restless, so I took them back down to the basement.

Sa Ron, in charge of the basement, took very good care of the animals, and he would groom the dogs every morning for ticks that he would discard into a bowl of water. They were always back the next day. He and the other guys slept on camp cots, and they would usually have their legs wrapped around a dog. A symbiotic relationship! Warmth and companionship for man and beast!

The Dog Holiday

I made friends with Jackie at work, and her Omani dog Gem. She had found him as an abandoned puppy around the back of her school, and adopted him. She didn't realize how much bigger he would grow as an adult dog, and ended up with a very large platinum blonde dog. We were talking at work about taking the dogs on a holiday, and another teacher, Alannah from Australia joined the conversation. So three women and two dogs went on a weekend trip to Koh Dach, or Silk Island. Alannah was a great help when we needed someone to hold the dogs' leashes for a minute.

A short ferry ride across the river, the island is a popular place for people wanting to get away from the noisy hustle and bustle of Phnom Penh. We booked three rooms at a guest house, with a French man and his Cambodian wife. He didn't tell us he had his own dog, who was quite territorial, but there was lots of room for the dogs upstairs where our rooms were.

Milo and Me in Tuk Tuk on Silk Island

We booked a tuk-tuk for the next day, and as we started out I put Milo down on the floor of the tuk-tuk as he was getting too big to be a lap dog. We drove all over the island, with its weaving communities and dirt roads. We stopped for lunch at a café right on the Mekong river and enjoyed cool drinks and snacks. The roads were quiet and safe, and we were rolling along peacefully when I realized Milo was licking Gem's privates! I expected a huge altercation but actually Gem seemed to be enjoying it! I put Milo on my bench to avoid conflict, just in case.

We spent a peaceful couple of days there, and then it was time to go back to the chaos of downtown Phnom Penh. Back in the city we stopped at a roundabout for traffic, and Milo leapt out of the tuk-tuk. I dashed after him as the traffic was backed up, and grabbed him by the collar. The whole incident was over in less than a minute.

The Second Dog Holiday

This time we took a long trip by taxi with the two dogs to Otres Beach to be able to enjoy the beach. This is the most popular beach near Sihanoukville. The area has now changed, as many high rise buildings have been built there by rich Chinese nationals. Many of these buildings are empty now, as the whole area was shut down due to Covid 19.

Another friend, Esme was staying nearby. She was visiting her Cambodian family in the area. I had stayed at the hotel a year before. This time we were doing it on the cheap, to accommodate the animals.

Our hotel was a budget version of the main hotel, Sok Sabay Resort. We had no refrigeration in the rooms, and any dog food left on the floor was quickly covered with ants. We quickly learned to ask if we could use the bar fridge. The price didn't include a swim in the hotel pool, even when Jackie offered to pay for her own swim. We were only paying seven dollars a night so we couldn't be too fussy. In the hotel last year we were given a welcome drink. Not this time! I felt annoyed that we were not allowed to use any of the amenities and were treated like second class citizens. Our little rooms were right on the river, and we could sit outside and enjoy the view. We were allowed to eat in the dining room though and the food was excellent.

The Beach!

One day we took a tuk-tuk to the beach. It was the first time Milo had ever been to a beach and I had never seen him so excited! He ran around in circles in the red mud, in and out of the surf, and his coat changed from a brown to a mahogany colour.

Luckily there were outdoor showers at our hotel for cleaning the dogs and also ourselves.

Jackie kept withdrawing from my company, and after I waited for her for over half an hour for dinner, I asked her where she was. "Emails!" was the reply. Most of the time I was on my own. Esme commented on this too. I asked her once to tell me more about her life, and she snapped, "I'm not going to recite." She said she would only tell me things "if they came up in conversation." I wasn't trying to pry, just to get to know her. She did tell me there was mental illness in her family.

On our way home in the taxi we stopped at a restaurant for lunch, and she and Gem sat at a table by themselves. From her body language I felt she didn't want me there. We finally made it back to Phnom Penh and it was good to be home.

Khmer Lessons

The school offered us free Khmer lessons once a week. I found it difficult, as my hearing isn't good any more.

The lessons were fun, and the Khmer teachers had many different methods of teaching us. We learned the basics, but I have forgotten most of the vocabulary. I did get 65 % on the final exam, which I felt was respectable, but there were much higher marks. I think my friend Jovan got a mark in the high 90's.

Laos Overview

Laos, or as the locals call it, Muang Lao, is a country of three kingdoms that was united in 1893 by the French Colonials. Since it was originally three kingdoms the "s" was added. In English the "s" is pronounced, but not in Lao.

Laos is a socialist state, officially the Lao People's Democratic Republic, and is the only land-locked country in Southeast Asia. It is bordered by Myanmar and China to the northwest, Vietnam to the east, Cambodia to the southeast, and Thailand to the west and southwest. Since there are no sea or river ports Laos generates electricity from its rivers and sells the power to its neighbours Thailand, China and Vietnam. Four new railways connect Laos to its neighbours. Credit to Wikipedia.

Trip to Laos

Julie and I had been planning a trip to Laos all term, and we booked a bus to go there when we had a mid-term break. I knew a couple who had gone there to retire, so we made plans to visit them in the "Four Thousand Islands." Lance is a musician with a long white beard braided and hanging down his chest. He and Donna met later in life and they are one of the happiest couples I know. We met them for dinner every night.

Photo of Lance and Donna in Laos

We stayed in that area for a few days, and then left for Pakse, with its wonderful rooftop restaurant. As in other countries in Southeast Asia, the local people were gracious and professional, and I felt safe there. The food was tasty and there was a lot to do: biking, swimming, reading and just lounging around. Julie wanted to go on a tour that included sleeping in the treetops, but when she tried to reserve a spot it was "Booked out." Julie is from Australia.

I enjoyed Laos so much that I went there for three different holidays. The last one was to the popular Luang Prabang. The entire city is a World Heritage Site, and it was a nice change to see the clean streets and hillsides.

Sticky Rice

Sticky rice is a staple food and has cultural and religious significance to the Lao people. It is preferred over jasmine rice and sticky rice cultivation is thought to have originated in Laos. There are many different traditions and rituals associated with rice production among many different ethnic groups.

One I found interesting is the practice of planting the rice variety khao kam. In Luang Prabang, the Khammu farmers plant this rice in small quantities near their farm house. This is done if their parents have passed away, but if their parents are still alive, the rice is planted at the edge of the rice field.

I would definitely recommend a trip to Laos for its diversity, its beauty and its lovely people.

Back to Cambodia

It was a very long bus ride back to Phnom Penh, so we decided to fly. The travel agent on Don Det told us we could fly back to Phnom Penh from Pakse. We couldn't. We could fly to Siem Reap though, and take another flight back to Phnom Penh from there. Exhausting!

Phnom Penh Pickpocketing!

The next Sunday Julie and I went swimming. We took a tuk-tuk, and I placed my bag on the seat beside me.

"No! Put it on the floor!" Yelled the driver, and I thought he was looking out for us, as there are a lot of bag snatching incidents in Phnom Penh.

He was talking to someone on the phone, and at that moment a snatch and grab happened to us- well, actually to me, as my bag was the one that was taken. There were two guys on the bike- one to drive- to slide in close enough for the other one to grab the bag. The passenger leaned over and quickly snatched my bag from the floor.

I wasn't upset at first, as all he got was a wet bathing suit that I could replace quite cheaply. But I forgot about my hearing aids- $1000 for foreigners. I was upset when I remembered! I paid for new ones in installments.

"At least they didn't get my phone, or my wallet" I thought. Later that day I was going out to a place I hadn't been to before, and I was on the phone looking for the address. Suddenly a moto swooped up, slid my purse off my arm and off he went. This time I filled out a police report, but never heard back from them.

It's such a common practice. I called Julie, who came right over with a big bottle of alcoholic comfort. She was wonderful, and didn't say anything about what an idiot I was and how I should have been paying more attention. I had already said these things to myself. Most of these thefts are done "For fun" by young boys of 15 or 16. Only an idiot would let this happen twice in one day!

I was watching a video on Cambodia on Youtube yesterday. They addressed this issue, and in BKK 1, Phnom Penh's most exclusive neighbourhood, there was a sign posted outside one of the lovely apartment buildings: "Beware Snatch Thief on the Street."

The War

A dark side of Cambodian history is the war and the genocide by the Khmer Rouge. Nearly a quarter of the population at the time, one and a half to two million people died from 1975 to 1979. Most of the people died in mass executions, and 20,000 were killed after passing through the Security Prison 21, or Toul Sleng. Prisoners were taken to the Killing Fields, where they were executed by garden hoes to save money on bullets and buried in mass graves. A chilling sight is the piles of skulls on display at Choeung Ek (The Killing Fields) and other memorials throughout the country. I saw a display in Battambang, with pictures of the instruments of torture. Other people died from malnutrition, physical abuse and disease.

Siem Reap has a lot of books about this horrendous time, and one of them, "First They Killed my Father," has been made into a movie directed by Angelina Jolie. Another book I would recommend is "The Tears of my Soul" by Reaksa Himm, the only survivor in his family of seven. His other two books are "After the Heavy Rain" and "Shepherd of my Soul" which gives tips on healing from PTSD: Post Traumatic Stress Disorder, using Psalm 23 as a guide. I first heard about Reaksa from Sophaly, his wife, who was in my ladies' bible study group. I bought the first book, which was a real page turner, and then the second and third ones. They are fascinating reading. Reaksa was interviewed recently on "100 Huntley Street," A Christian program in Toronto.

My Tattoo

One morning I looked in the mirror and part of my left eyebrow was missing! I decided to get a tattoo if it was safe and not too expensive. On my last trip back to BC I went to a shopping mall in Maple Ridge with my friend Ginny. There was a big sign advertising eyebrow tattoos, but the cost was prohibitive- $400!

Back in Cambodia I was chatting to my boss Visal as we climbed the stairs. He asked me if I had any tattoos, and I said the only one I would be interested in was an eyebrow tattoo. He recommended one his wife had used, near the Central Market. After looking at hundreds of photos I chose one that I thought would suit me.

The cost was $150 USD, and this was for three appointments. I was very nervous the first day, but the ladies there were reassuring and professional. I chose one out of the book of many samples they showed me. It was thin and natural looking. One of them slathered a thick gel on my brows; this was the pain reliever. They kept reapplying it. and the process took a long time. It only hurt a little, when the woman was using the needle, and my next appointment wasn't for another month. They took my photo right away, and I suppose it was added to the hundreds already in stock.

The second and third time I went there I felt a lot of pain. Maybe it was because they didn't leave the gel on for a long time. I was relieved when it was all over after three months. I was very happy with the result, and in spite of the pain I was glad I did it, but I can't understand why people want to deface other parts of their bodies with a painful, expensive procedure. To each his own!

ACE

Even though I had taught there for a year and a half my contract was not renewed. My boss Visal said I was "Good, but not good enough."

One demo class went very well, and my observer said it did, but she would just have to check with Visal. The next time I saw her the smile was gone, and she said it wasn't good enough. There was a theme for the lesson and I didn't stick to it, even though the class was lively and motivated. I had prepared lots of fun activities for them to enjoy.

I was disappointed, but I decided to try my luck at other schools. My visa was going to expire in July and I started looking for an apartment in another neighbourhood. I found a beautiful place near Toul Sleng, the genocide museum. The new landlord checked off items on a list, and Sodet and his friends came to help with the translation. It was always a problem moving out of an apartment in Cambodia, because the owners would try and squeeze as much money out of the damage deposit as possible. Extra charges such as garbage pickup and water were added to the bill. There was a question about something in my previous apartment, but I was not to blame. I suggested to my previous landlord that he make a similar list of items at the beginning and end of the tenancy.

My Beautiful Balcony.
It was only a couple of
blocks from my school.
I signed a contract for
a year.

One of the reasons I took the apartment was the landlord, who was extremely nice and welcoming. I didn't realize he would change his colours at the end.

The best feature of my new apartment was the balcony off the bedroom. It had wicker chairs and potted palms. Unfortunately it was too hot to sit out there except in the very early mornings. It was fully furnished, including bedding and drapes, and cost about $480 which included maid service twice a week.

I really liked the area. It was close to coffee shops, bars and restaurants, and also the Flicks Community Theatre, which had movies for $2.00. If you wanted to you could stay all day and watch three movies for no extra charge. What a deal! It was not a big place, and only seats 30 people., but they would serve hot popcorn to people in their seats! It ran until last year, 2021, and has now, sadly closed for good. I saw a lot of good films there, with or without friends, and I am sure it will be missed by a lot of people.

I also lived within walking distance of my church, and my friend Esme, who had a room at a charity across the street. We would often meet for lunch. She liked the "Spider" restaurant, but we didn't have any as there were lots of other choices.

Milo on the roof waiting for me to rescue him.

Milo- Lost!

There was a small restaurant on the street below my apartment, and I got into the habit of having breakfast there early in the morning. Milo would sit under the table. One morning I let him off the leash and he ran down the street. People were asking me about him, and I said,

"Oh, he'll be back", as he had done this before and always returned in a few minutes. Not this time. When he didn't come back in 15 minutes, I starting walking down the street, expecting to see him any minute. I called and called, and heard a soft whimper, but couldn't see him anywhere, until I looked up and saw him on the roof of one of the houses, which were all two-stories. A lot of these homes didn't have air conditioners, and left the bottom door open. My theory is that Milo chased a cat up the stairs and couldn't find his way down!

He was running back and forth along the roofs, as they were all connected. I went to borrow a small plastic chair so I could reach up and catch him, but he's over 30 pounds and I was afraid of falling. Then a man who was opening his shop next door got another small chair, stood on it and we both caught Milo as he jumped down. The corrugated roof is still slightly bent where he jumped.

Attempted Murder!

Farm to Table is a very popular restaurant among expats in Phnom Penh, with its tasty food, live entertainment, and dog friendly policy. The problem is, they have live chickens running around on the dirt floor. I had Milo with me one night, and we were with some friends. I had him on the leash, wrapped over my hand. Suddenly it was pulled out of my hand, when Milo pounced on a chicken pecking its way past our table. Milo had the bird IN HIS MOUTH! It was hanging limply from his jaws. One of the staff grabbed the chicken, put it on a plate and took it to an empty room at the back. It wasn't moving. It lay limply on the plate. I was mortified.

We were discussing how much I would have to pay for the chicken- $7, and I was trying to peek into the room at the back when a staff member came out and said the chicken had recovered! We watched it strutting by our table a couple of minutes later. Maybe it was playing dead!

Looking for Another Job

There are lots of English schools in Phnom Penh, so I didn't think I would have any trouble finding another job. It wasn't meant to be, even though I had a few interviews. Maybe it was my age. I was very excited when I met a woman at church, who told me they were looking for someone at their school. I hadn't heard of it so I asked Sodet, who told me it was "The best school in Phnom Penh." It was a Christian school that focused on art courses. I went to the interview, and the woman I had met was there, as she was one of the department heads. Afterwards, she said that she thought I did well, but I didn't get the job. I said that I was a Christian, but the woman in charge "wanted more."

I was offered two jobs. One was at an elementary school nearby, and my landlord's daughter attended it. The schedule was very busy, with five or six classes every day, so I turned it down. I didn't think I had the energy.

The other one was a lovely kindergarten where my friend Mirasol teaches art. When I told them I was leaving in a couple of months they said they wanted someone long term. An NGO called "Aziza's Place" didn't hire me for the same reason.

Bony

I found a girl who was looking for a tutor, and I spent the last few weeks in Cambodia tutoring her. She and her fiance were planning to get married and move to the USA, where he practices law. I found a lot of English teaching websites on my phone, and we used these to practice colloquial English.

Bony is now living in the USA, and is the mother of a very cute little boy. I wish her and her family all the best!

House of Hounds

Every morning I would take Milo to the doggie day care: House of Hounds. It had a variety of different dogs, and he made friends with a couple of them. We walked there from my place, and sometimes I would stop for coffee at the many take away places enroute.

But by the time I went to pick him up at 2 pm it was too hot to walk, and I would take a tuk-tuk to pick him up. It was $7 for half a day and $10 for a full day. He boarded there when I went to Laos again, and I got a lot of dog care advice from them. Trevor, the co-owner was a former military man in Papua New Guinea, and had lots of interesting stories to tell.

He recommended a good vet, and also where to find a good travel agent. The vet, Chamnan Nou, was only a couple of streets over from my home. A big grey cat lay on her counter teasing the dogs that came in. Milo tried to jump and catch her but she was out of reach and she knew it.

When Chamnan filled out the paperwork for travel she wrote "Cambodian Short Hair" next to "Breed". I said I didn't know that breed, and she said,

"Sounds better than street dog."

It was easy to relocate Milo to Canada. No chips or passport. Just a lot of paperwork and of course the shots. My mistake was not getting him used to the crate he was going to travel in, and it was a very traumatic experience for him.

Chapter 12

Leaving Cambodia

When I went to Palm Travel I asked about the three pet-friendly airlines, and were told they were all very expensive. I asked the travel agent to keep on looking. Neither one of us thought to check the visa requirements. After all, I was going back to my home country. What could possibly go wrong? She called me a couple of weeks later to say that Philippine Airlines were cheaper, and she could get me a ticket to Vancouver with a stopover in Manila. I told her to book it, not realizing I would be detained in Manila for four days!

My departure day was July 19, and I wanted to save time, so I went to my landlord to settle up my bill. I paid him for the damage Milo had done to the door- scratching at the glass and leaving marks on it. He was very pleasant, and even invited me for dinner.

The day of my departure was a different story. He came to my place in the afternoon, and seemed to be in a bad mood. I gave him some dishes I couldn't take with me, and he didn't even thank me. He said he would be back later to repay my damage deposit.

Sodet and Voleak came along with Sodet's friend, to translate. Mr. Sin, my landlord came up, and seemed really upset. He pulled my bed apart, and there was a small spot of bleach on the sheet. He said my dog had bitten the sheet, and he would have to buy a new mattress. He said he was going to take $50 off my damage deposit! I was very upset but said nothing. I think his wife had told him to do this to get more money out of me.

When we left I forgot to take my degrees and certificates in a folder, and I emailed Sodet about it. He said he called Mr. Sin and he said he threw the papers away. So much for my nice landlord!

Soksan, my driver the last few months, came in his brand-new car to pick us up, and told me not to pay him for the trip. I gave Sodet $20 to give him later. Soksan also gave me a beautiful bouquet of fresh flowers. I gave this to the woman helping with Milo. There were more forms to fill out for him for international travel. She told me I would be able to see him in Manila, when they let the dogs out for exercise. It was only a four-hour flight to Manila, and a stopover for seven hours.

Marooned in Manila

When we landed in Manila it was very crowded, and when I showed the woman at the desk my British passport which I had been using, as I was born in England, she asked me about my Canadian passport. I showed it to her but it had expired. She told me to enter Canada I needed a valid Canadian passport, as the rules had changed, but she would write a letter, and I may not need to. She said to come to the airport early.

Disheartened, I went to look for Milo, and where to find the area with the dogs. Well he was the only one on the flight, and I was directed to the luggage pick up. After a few minutes, his crate came up out of the bowels of the airport. He was very excited to see me, but had soiled himself and he smelled terrible. I had bought him a brand-new water bottle for the trip, and he had chewed it to pieces. I took him and all my bags to the ladies' washroom to try to clean his cage.

"I do it", said a lovely looking girl working in the washroom and she proceeded to clean and sanitize his crate. I wanted to contact someone to commend her for her good service, but they said, "We don't do that here." I went to look for her later on but she was off duty. Her friend was there, though, and we called her and chatted.

I took a taxi to the hotel I had booked, and quickly found out they didn't allow dogs! One of the desk clerks said I should speak to the guys outside. I did, and they said they would look after Milo for the afternoon and they also gave him a bath! I tipped them $10 for their help.

When I got to the room I wearily looked around, counted my bags and then realized I was missing one of my them! Luckily we were close to the airport, so I took a taxi there and found the missing bag. It had started raining, and I had to wait in line and provide a credit card to use the Grab back to the hotel. I started to feel stressed out, but was still hoping to get on the flight.

After a short nap I went to collect Milo, who had been very well taken care of with the outside staff. Back we went to the airport and the moment of truth. The girl there told me there had been no response to her letter asking if I could board the flight. She offered to keep trying, and I spent my time praying that we would be able to board. We were there for several hours, and I had to take Milo outside a couple of times past security and all the passengers entering the doors. I found out they had only changed the rules one month previously, and I hadn't contacted the Canadian government before travelling. This was the travel agent's job, but I guess she didn't think I would have a problem entering my own country. Wrong!

I told my story to several different Phillipine Airline personnel, but they were unable to help me. They said I would have to apply for and obtain a new passport before I could go back to Canada! The worst moment was when I was crossing the terminal and saw a group of foreigners through the glass. They were boarding my flight!

So there I was with Milo, and one of the girls gave me a post-it note with the name of a hotel on it.

"They take dogs." She said.

So with this information I went outside to find a taxi. It was raining, but I thought I would soon be ensconced in a cosy hotel and be able to sleep. We went to the hotel. They didn't take dogs and they didn't know any hotel that did. We drove around and around, and went to at least six other hotels. None of them were pet friendly, and the raindrops on the window mirrored my tears of frustration.

Finally the driver said he said he knew a place that would take a dog. Really? We went past a sign with an unusual logo: a woman with her finger over her lips in a hushing gesture. The hotel was called Victoria Court. We had to check in downstairs, and then climb up a flight of stairs to the windowless room. Then I understood the logo. It was a love hotel! There was a little entranceway at the top, so the delivery person couldn't see into the room. It was very nice, with a jacuzzi in the bathroom and 24-hour room service. And there were very interesting programs on tv to get you "In the Mood."

The bed was very comfortable, and the food was tasty. Milo shared it with me. The next day however, I had to go all the way across town to the Canadian Embassy. The taxi was $50 USD. Then I had to surrender my phone and wait in line.

The woman on the desk said I would have to provide them with three phone numbers in Canada to verify my story. She was not very friendly. I resented this because I have always been an honest person. One of my Facebook friends pointed out that thousands of refugees are allowed into Canada with no documentation. There was nothing I could do, and my friend Ginny was very helpful and provided them with the information.

The second day I was able to fill out an application for a temporary passport, and I found out how to take public transportation to get there. I had to go to another building to get a photo taken and met a woman on the street who helped me. She was an opera singer and gave me her website address.

The staff at the hotel were very helpful and friendly, and Milo was a big hit with everyone. Crowds were everywhere, and though I had been to Manila before the crush of people and the noise was overwhelming. We stayed close to the hotel.

We stayed in Manila for four days, until I was granted my temporary passport, and booked my flight back to Vancouver. After my long flight "Across the pond" I finally arrived back in Canada. My faithful friend Ginny was there to pick me up, and it was so good to see her and be back in my homeland!

As I look back on my experiences overseas I don't have any regrets, and would do this again if I had a chance. If anyone thinks they are too old or feel too afraid to travel and experience another country, go for it! I once took a course called "Feel the Fear and do it Anyway", based on the book by Melody Beattie. It seems at the end of life people don't regret what they did as much as what they didn't do.

My life hasn't been easy, but I always come through the hard times. I give credit to the Lord Jesus for protecting me through the challenging times. Searching out Christian communities gave me a lot of support and a lot of lovely friendships.

I also want to thank my lovely friends and family for their support. On to the next adventure!

Printed in the USA
CPSIA information can be obtained
at www.ICGtesting.com
JSHW071904101024
71342JS00007B/11